TELEVANGELISM

The Marketing of Popular Religion

Razelle Frankl

Southern Illinois University Press
Carbondale and Edwardsville

Library of Congress Cataloging-in-Publication Data

Frankl, Razelle, 1932–
   Televangelism: the marketing of popular religion.

   Bibliography: p.
   Includes index.
   1. Television in religion—United States.   2. United
States—Church history—20th century.   I. Title.
BV656.3.F73   1987   306'.6   86-6584
ISBN 0-8093-1299-9

For Victor Steven,
child of the '60s, victim of the '70s

Dedicated to my loving family,
Bill, Brian, and Rachel,
who continue to give meaning to my life

CONTENTS

Part Four
The Electric Church

Appendixes

ILLUSTRATIONS

Plates

Figures

TABLES

FOREWORD

Every now and then someone comes along and examines a problem from a fresh perspective, and with that perspective changes the way we understand the problem. Such is the case with Razelle Frankl's investigation of the phenomenon of televangelism. Her inquiry into the source and nature of religious broadcasting has transformed dramatically the way I think about the electric church. I am confident that the insights developed here will significantly influence how others think about the subject.

Frankl focuses her inquiry on the social organization of the predecessors of the "electric church," tracing the roots of modern televangelism to nineteenth-century urban revivalism. To the student of American church history, this is not an altogether novel idea. In the early days of his revival crusades, Billy Graham was often compared to Billy Sunday, the last of the great urban revivalists. Nevertheless, while this lineage has been recognized, until now no one has ever taken more than passing note. Frankl shows us *how* the nineteenth-century phenomenon of urban revivalism is linked to late-twentieth-century televangelism; in the process, she demonstrates *why* this lineage is so important. Through her analysis we witness the gradual unfolding of an organizational form that may well be transforming America.

The major televangelists exhibit important differences in style and in the structures of their organizations, but a critical thread traverses them all: they all stand as autonomous units. Organized on the principles of free enterprise, their hierarchical structures are essentially oligarchic. Supersalesmen all, the televangelists are free to pursue just about any project they want so long as they can convince their audiences that it is worthwhile. They have neither bishops, nor presbyteries, nor general conferences, nor burdensome bureaucracies to hold them back when they feel the Lord is calling them to pursue a new venture. Frankl argues that this autonomous form did not emerge *de novo*. It evolved gradually, most of its unique organizational features deriving from similarly autonomous urban revival organizations.

Charles Grandison Finney (1792–1875) is credited with being the father of modern revivalism. Finney's contribution was the *rationalization* of the revival. Finney's conviction that one ought to be able to apply principles of logical persuasion to the art of winning souls was a direct extension of his training as a lawyer. But it was also an application of techniques of rational persuasion and social organization that anticipated by half a century Frederick Taylor's "principles of scientific management."

While he was creating new techniques of revivalism, Finney was also radically restructuring American theology. Although he did not initiate it, he significantly intensified a process begun by John Wesley and others who departed from the Calvinist doctrine of predestination. Finney believed that salvation was not predetermined, but rather rested with the free will of every mortal: everyone, in this view, is free to receive or reject God's gift of salvation. Finney's goal was to create an environment that would enhance the chances of people making the right decision.

Dwight L. Moody (1837–99) was a businessman who "bought" Finney's radical theology and applied the knowledge and techniques of the salesman to encourage mortals to make the right decision. For Moody it was a straightforward sales proposition—eternal life in exchange for acknowledging Christ's gift of salvation and his lordship over one's life. But there was more. Moody saw great urgency in bringing as many souls as possible to Christ before it was too late. Thus, in preparing for revivals Moody bypassed denominational and local church authority, appealing to local businessmen for financial resources. Once he had obtained their cooperation, it was difficult for local religious authorities not to join in.

New religious bodies had long been formed by sectarian schism from established churches; Moody achieved a new form of autonomous ecclesiastical authority without schism. Many did not particularly like the autonomous *parachurch* institution that Moody created, but they were not in a strong position to oppose his activities. Ironically, Moody fostered and built interdenominational cooperation even as his parachurch structures undermined the authority of denominations. That same irony persists today in the electric church.

Billy Sunday (1863–1935) rationalized the process of urban revival to an even greater degree and added the important element of entertainment and, later, explicit patriotism. But by the end of the first quarter of this century urban revivalism had apparently run its course. Fundamentalism, which had come to be the principal message of the revivalists, suffered a serious setback at the hands of Clarence Darrow during the Scopes trial. Relatively speaking, urban revivalism was dormant during the second quarter of this century, but the advent of radio provided a medium in which the essential character of revivalism would survive. Charles Fuller was the most important figure in keeping alive and transforming the parachurch structures of urban revivalism. He was followed in the late 1940s by Billy Graham, who was soon using both radio and television to give new impetus to urban revivalism. But the task of transforming revivalism into the electric church fell to two Pentecostal tent revivalists from the Southwest, Oral Roberts and Rex Humbard.

In *Science and Human Values,* Jacob Bronowski speaks of science as the search for "unity in hidden likenesses." Once the hidden likenesses are uncovered, they seem so obvious that it is sometimes difficult to recognize that anything new has been discovered. As one who has struggled for a number of years to understand the origins of modern televangelism, I stand as witness to the significance of Razelle Frankl's discovery of hidden likeness. Not only has Frankl found the roots of modern televangelism, she has also provided the essential components for understanding how urban revivalism was transformed in the late 1970s into the New Christian Right. This insight, based on Frankl's broader historical analysis, provides concrete evidence for the proposition that the New Christian Right is more than a passing phase in the life of fundamentalism, more than a fading movement on the margin of American culture.

The notion that fundamentalism and evangelical Protestantism are about to expire is comforting to those who would rather not deal with the fact that many in our culture hold their religious beliefs with deep conviction. But the comforting myth does not match reality, and the reality should not be ignored. No other interest group has greater access to the airwaves than do the syndicated religious broadcasters, who are almost exclusively fundamentalists and evangelicals. They stand positioned, as never before, to proselytize both their religious and their political-economic views.

Frankl has a truly profound grasp of the central tendencies that have formed this new style of religion, and her work must be considered an important addition to the handful of studies on the electric church. Although many more studies will certainly follow, *Televangelism* will no doubt be recognized as a seminal influence on our understanding of religious broadcasting.

JEFFREY K. HADDEN

ACKNOWLEDGMENTS

I would like to thank Dick and Liz Ostrander, whose serendipitous remarks led me to discover the phenomenon of religious television. Their warm friendship and wise counsel contributed to this study.

I thank Jeffrey K. Hadden for his sage comments and suggestions on my dissertation, which guided me in writing this book. I am indebted to Jeffrey K. Hadden and Charles Swann for the hybrid word televangelism first used in *Primetime Preachers;* and to the Society for the Scientific Study of Religion which provided many opportunities for me to present my ideas.

I thank the faculty in the Department of Sociology at Bryn Mawr, whose wise encouragement led me to realize, as Molière's "Bourgeois Gentilhomme" did, that I had been speaking sociology all my life. I especially thank Eugene V. Schneider, whose critical eye and personal assurances served his mentoring role, encouraging me to express with conviction my scholarly achievements. Professor Schneider with his humanistic and scientific values served as a model for my professional development. I also thank in particular Judith Porter, whose course in Sociology of Religion led me to a "new" area, which provided the mortar for my long-term interest in organizations and their goals. Sociology of religion provided the substance I had been missing in organizational analysis.

I thank with great appreciation my fellow sociology students and other graduate students for their wise advice and their emotional support during the years of solitary labor. Over the years, they have become valued friends and professional colleagues. I especially want to thank Edith Gross, Ann Jenkins, and Susan Thomson, who were always helpful and willing to ponder with me innumerable puzzles encountered during the research of this book. I would like to thank Cindy Koneco and Nora Dempsey, whose assistance in the computer laboratory was very much appreciated; Wood Boulden, resident evangelist and graduate student, for his critical insights into the dynamics of revivalist preaching; Rita Buckley Connolly, for her skillful assistance with my fieldwork; and Beth Milke, whose assistance and professional training were invaluable in the development of the content analysis techniques and conceptualization.

I would like to thank Gary Calore and Seth Fagin, coders of exceptional integrity and perserverence, who made a tedious process enjoyable and whose work assured me that my findings were indeed reliable. On their hard and competent work, my confidence in the data collection rests.

A very special thank you to Ullik Rouk, for her professional guidance in transforming a dissertation into a book.

Of course, I am indebted to Diane Weinstock, my typist of infinite patience. Thank you for your help.

This work could not have been sustained without the help of my family. I owe thanks to my son Brian and my daughter Rachel for urging me to finish, and Brian also for his research at the Moody Bible Institute. Especially to Bill, who has always encouraged my scholarship, I owe the most sincere and loving thank you.

And to Victor Steven, who always told me not to give up. I finish this while missing him.

PART I

THE CONCEPT OF THE ELECTRIC CHURCH

1

INTRODUCTION TO THE ELECTRIC CHURCH

> The unprecedented linking of twentieth-century technology with Christ's commandment, "Go ye into all the world, and preach the gospel to every creature" (Mark 16:15), has created a dynamic new phenomenon that I call "the electric church."
>
> (Armstrong, 1979:8)

EVERY SUNDAY MORNING, nearly 130 million Americans, according to Ben Armstrong, tune their radio and television sets to the "electric church." The terms refers to commercial religious programs produced for television and radio by evangelical and usually fundamentalist organizations. Armstrong is executive director of the National Religious Broadcasters (NRB), the trade association of the religious broadcast industry. One of the primary missions on the association's agenda is to increase the use of television and radio for transmission of the gospel (Armstrong, 1979).

By naming this gathering of listeners and viewers the "electric church," Armstrong, in effect, gave it a life of its own and a legitimacy as a viable social phenomenon. But the electric church is far more than a "religious gathering." It is a significant organizational development comprising five religious broadcast networks, more than sixty syndicated television programs, and an ever-expanding number of television and radio stations owned by religious groups. Moreover, this phenomenon has become a major sociopolitical movement of our time.

3

Televangelists such as Jerry Falwell, Pat Robertson, and James Robison have become opinion leaders for the New Christian Right, both on and off their television programs. No longer primarily in the business of saving souls, the electric church is, to use LaHaye's term, fighting the "battle of the mind." There is no doubt that this Sunday-morning gathering plays a key role in the social and political agenda of the New Right and was instrumental in the election of Ronald Reagan as president. Its influence continues in the policies of the Reagan administration and in the Republican congressional leadership.

The history of the electric church and the use of mass communications to preach the gospel can be traced to modern revivalism as developed in the nineteenth century by Charles Grandison Finney, Dwight Moody, and Billy Sunday, with their novel techniques of bringing the gospel to the urban centers of America. As we shall see, these three men established the roles, the forms, and the messages of urban revivalism. Much of the fundamentalist-modernist split within American Protestantism stems from the theology expressed in their preaching. Their most important legacy, however, was their revivalist ethos, or use of "appropriate means" to stir religious enthusiasm.

The more recent surge of interest in the electric church has been bolstered, in large measure, by the turbulent social climate of the past three decades. This era has been characterized by economic growth and abundance, yet accompanied by dislocations in employment patterns—chronic high unemployment and the increasing entrance of women into the workforce—as well as by rapidly changing norms of behavior and values. Antimilitary protests, flagrant sexuality, widespread drug abuse, rising numbers of abortions, a growing incidence of venereal disease, and climbing divorce rates are only a few of the indicators fundamentalists point to as symbols of contemporary social and moral decay and irreligiousness. These conditions, television preachers tell their followers, are the product of secular humanism, or "man's attempt to solve his problems independently of God" (LaHaye, 1980:26). In the course of their religious preaching, these television ministries provide much material around which their listeners can be exhorted to a fervent religiosity (Falwell, 1980; LaHaye, 1980).

While these cultural and religious values are divisive, it is the issue of using mass-communications technology to spread religious messages that separates proponents of the electric church from antagonists. Although mainstream religions have long employed religious broadcasting, both in the United States and in foreign missionary work, these broadcasts have not, in and of themselves, been the primary thrust of their organizational activities. The commercial nature of religious programs and their competition for air time and viewers tends to offend mainstream religious groups, many of whom are already unsympathetic to fundamentalist theology.

This book argues that the present popularity of conservative philosophy, coupled with the use of television, a complex and structured communications technology, accounts for the new formats, message changes, and role modifications that distinguish the electric church from urban revivalism. The outcome is a new social-religious institution—a hybrid of revivalism and television—which is quantitatively and qualitatively different from the social institution of revivalism. In order to understand this phenomenon, we must go beyond the electric church's own rhetoric and hyperbole to look objectively at what this new institution is and does.

The Objectives of the Electric Church

One of the first questions regarding any social institution concerns its goals and objectives. What are the results of its activities? Armstrong holds that one of the purposes of the electric church is to unify Christians and to "revitalize the older forms of the churches, empowering them to keep up with the twentieth-century challenges of a rapidly diminishing time span before the return of Jesus Christ" (1979:11). He voices the sentiments of his entire religious broadcasting community when he states his belief "that God has raised up this powerful technology of radio and television expressly to reach every man, woman, boy, and girl on earth with the even more powerful message of the gospel" (1979:7). Armstrong cites as his major objective a change in the lives of his listeners and viewers. "The larger the audience, the greater the response in terms of lives changed. That is the major objective of religious broadcasting and the only meaningful measurement of success of any ministry" (1979:137).

If Armstrong's hypothesis—the greater the number of listeners and viewers, the greater the number of lives changed—is true, then it would appear that religious broadcasters are getting their messages out effectively indeed. They are reaching vast audiences: Armstrong claims as many as 130 million viewers and listeners. Yet this claim has been widely disputed. Other early estimates range from a high of about 35 million viewers and listeners (Martin, 1980) to a low of 20.5 million (Hadden and Swann, 1981). Later estimates, in the Annenberg/Gallup Study of Religion and Television (Gerbner et al., 1984), also presented contradictory reports of estimated audience size. Annenberg maintained that the religious television audience is relatively small (6.2 percent of the total television audience), while Gallup claimed that one in three viewers watch religious broadcasts (32 percent of the total). These contradictions are difficult to resolve. New Nielsen data, however, reported by Clark and Virts (1985) supports the Gallup findings. Putting this argument aside for the moment, Armstrong attributes much of the success of the electric church to the broadcasters' skill in adapting the medium or in "matching the message to fit the medium" (Armstrong, 1979:89). This match, Armstrong asserts, has been responsible for changing "the way Christians understood their relationship to God and the way they expressed their devotion through worship" (1979:10–11).

But Armstrong acknowledges that there are negative aspects to the electric church. One is the high cost of broadcasting; another is the change in relationship among the members caused by the "absence of the *koinonia,* the gathering together in community of believers" (1979:9). Nonetheless, Armstrong dismisses the latter, stating that the broadcasters urge viewers to attend church as a way of filling the void. The weak link, he charges, arises from the churches themselves because they do not adequately serve their members. Thus, he claims that the electric church is not vying with local churches for members (a major contention of mainstream congregations), but rather that it is a phenomenon that transcends established churches. According to Armstrong, the listeners and viewers of religious broadcasts are "the members of the great and new manifestation of the church created by God for this age—the electric church" (1979:9). The act of worshipping at home is merely "a reversal of roles," with the outcome "a revolution as dramatic as the revolution that began when Martin Luther nailed his ninety-five theses to the cathedral door at Wittenberg" (1979:10).

"Electric" versus "Electronic" Church

The term *electric* in *electric church* is generally used in a dual sense. *Electric* refers to the electricity that physically transmits the church message and to the electrifying effect religious broadcasters have on the audiences. As used in this book, however, the term *electric church* refers to a much broader concept, one that takes in the entire message system, including the organizations producing the broadcasts, the audiences viewing them, and the messages sent (Gerbner, 1966a; 1975). Described in this manner, the electric church consists of considerably more than just religious television and radio programs. It encompasses a complete social institution with defined organizations, a variety of occupations and roles, and a set of beliefs and values. Its goal is to produce a special and new type of Christian commercial broadcast, espousing evangelical-fundamentalist theological, social, and sometimes even political positions to mass audiences.

Electronic church refers to the same phenomenon as *electric church,* but the former is used by nonmembers, who are often critical of this new development. William Fore, assistant general secretary of communications for the National Council of the Churches of Christ, defines the electronic church as "those programs that present a preacher and a religious service and that are aimed at creating a strong, loyal group of followers to the preachers and service" (quoted in Hadden, 1980b). A more comprehensive and less evaluative definition of the electronic church is presented by Hadden (1980), who includes "all electronic communication that is generally perceived by senders and receivers alike as religious in intent and content."

Of all the terms in this discussion, it is the concept of "church" which is the most ambiguous and misleading. Armstrong's usage raises serious questions, for it implies a redefinition of the sociological and theological concepts of church. In the sociological typology of church-sect (see Moberg, 1962), this new form of worshipping, witnessing in the home, seems to be inappropriate. "Church" is used in the traditional church-sect sense implies an established organizational form, with members meeting for worship in a set building or place. Johnson (1971), however, argues that this typology, derived from Weber, was never applicable to the American religious context in the first place because it was historically specific. With this reasoning, the term *church* appears to be even less applicable to the electric church or television ministry.

At the Consultation on the Electronic Church, Fr. Richard P. McBrien, Professor of Theology at Boston College, enumerated six conditions in an ecclesiastical definition of *church:*

(1) There is a corporate confession of the Lordship of Jesus; (2) that confession of faith is ratified in Baptism, the Eucharist, or Lord's Supper, and other sacraments; (3) there is regular nourishment on the biblical word of God as a force that summons the

community of faith; (4) there is a sense of fellowship within the group, i.e., a common awareness of the call to become a community; (5) there is an acceptance of the Gospel of Jesus Christ as the conscious motivation for the community's values and ethical commitment; and (6) there exist certain formal ministries which are designed and exercised to assist the community in remaining faithful to its mission and for providing order, coherence, and stability to its internal life so that the community really can be a sacrament of Christ and of the Kingdom of God. (McBrien, 1980:3)

According to McBrien, the electronic church does not meet the second criterion, "sacramental dimension to their worship," or the fourth criterion, "meaningful sense of being a particular community in Christ" (1980:4). McBrien distinguished between *watching* a celebration of the Eucharist and *participating* in it (1980:5).

McBrien's theological criticism is in keeping with general usage of the term *church* as a place of worship, or a service at a church building. It is the communal act for some religious or transcendental purpose which, up to now, has distinguished a church for most individuals. McBrien's interpretation echoes Durkheim's basic concept of religion as a society or group whose members "are united by the fact that they think the same way in regard to the sacred world and its relations with the profane world, and by the fact that they translate these *common ideas* into common practices" (Durkheim, 1965:59; italics added).

The Sociological Question

Armstrong's position is that the expression *electric church* applies merely to the use of technology in the ritual of worship. It is not a new social institution but a continuation of nineteenth-century fundamentalism in modern-day dress. Yet the electric church has given birth to a new "social construction of reality" for those people who are its members. Instead of being a successful use and expansion of religious broadcasting, the evidence shows that we have an entirely new type of "church," a new institution stimulated and created with the use of television technology.

This phenomenon offers an opportunity to study a developing institution whose activities raise important substantive issues—issues such as the role of mass media in the structural differentiation of religious institutions and the connection between religion and politics. Some of the questions to which we seek answers are: How has the institution of revivalism been altered, and specifically, what changes can be seen? What new social structures and roles have been developed for the preacher, his relationship with his audience, and the organization which produces his "show" in response to the use of television? In what ways has the revivalist message itself been altered? Do we have an example of adaptation or social transformation when we examine the electric church?

This study examines the general sociological development of the electric church as a social institution, the nature of its relationships with other institutions, its political goals, and the influence of television on its messages. Answering the many questions raised requires finding the proper sociological lens. A close-up, which simply shows who watches television religion or what messages are being sent but which otherwise lacks theoretical focus, is useful to a degree. But the reasoned concern by Hadden and Swann (1981) about the link between the televangelists and the New Right needs sharper focus, as do a number of other significant issues. For this, we need a perspective that will enable us to grasp the basic nature of the electric church.

In two institutional worlds, religion and television, where does the electric church fit? Although called a "church," it does not appear classifiable as one since, among other reasons, the minister/congregant relationship is mediated by an impersonal technology. How can meaningful comparisons be made to gauge competition between the electric church and local churches? Membership in the electric church means turning on the television set and sending in money. Can this be compared, on any level, with attending a church service? What are the meaningful equivalents?

The same questions occur in classifying the electric church as broadcasting. Although its leaders are part of the television industry, they are treated as religious organizations by the Federal Communications Commission (Lacey, 1978). They are mass communicators entrusted with access to the airways, which they use to transmit their personal definition of social reality and of religious truth. What in this situation are the meaningful terms of comparison? Commercial television sells soap and hamburgers, while religious television sells redemption and salvation.

Where in the substantive traditions in sociology of religion and sociology of mass communications do we place the "electric church"? The sociologist's task is to compare the object of study with similar objects in order to classify and analyze similarities and differences. As a sociological technique, Mills recommends examining comparative and historical social structures:

> To become aware of problems of structure, and of the explana-
> tory significance for even individual behavior, requires a much
> broader style of empiricism . . . that variety, and hence the very
> formulation of problems, becomes available only when our view
> is broadened to include comparative and historical social struc-
> tures. (1972:68)

We shall apply Mills's recommendation to the study of the electric church. The ideal type of social structures in urban revivalism (roles, types of messages and types of men who led these religious events) will serve as one basis for our comparative analysis. By comparing the modern electric church with nineteenth-century revivalism, we can distinguish what is merely tradition and continuity from what is new. Second, we can witness the presence of social structural change. Galt and Smith explain how this operates in social-science models: "To understand change in a particular phenomenon it must be viewed at 2 points in time, at the very least, and the process of change inferred. The observations at particular points in time may be synchronic or static observations" (1976:37).

It is the function of the analysis of the ideal type of urban revivalism to yield one point in time for our institutional comparison with the electric church. As we analyze the electric church today, we shall want to see if there are changes in social structures, their components, and the relationships among the component parts (Mills, 1972:150).

The study of television as an institution also requires shifting from one perspective to another. A historical lens shows the televison industry emerging as a provider of entertainment into a highly bureaucratic, technology-dependent social system in the business of selling products with techniques of mass persuasion (Barnouw, 1978; Merton, 1946; Reardon, 1981). It is, simultaneously, a production system which "manufactures" popular ideas and images. A different lens is required to view the nature of this production system and its influence on the television program. This lens will allow us to observe and analyze the sequence of images that the producer places on the screen. This, in turn, will enable us to define his religious message.

On one level, we are taking the historical-comparison approach in order to understand the changes that were required for the institution of urban revivalism to become the electric church. This historical-comparison approach also helps us to understand the "religious" nature of the electric church. Here we are using the long-range lens, so to speak. On another level, understanding television and its influence on the content of its shows requires a much more close-up analysis. This kind of analysis correlates themes and messages with the teleministries producing them. Only in this dual manner can we define and understand this hybrid institution called the "electric church."

2

STUDIES OF THE ELECTRIC CHURCH

The members of the electric church differ dramatically from the critics' stereotypes of alienated loners who can't relate to others. As a matter of record, it's the eager outreach of the electric church that has carried religious radio from the pioneer years of the crystal set and on to new achievements.

(Armstrong, 1979:22)

ARMSTRONG IS CLEARLY AN ADVOCATE of the electric church. As leader of the National Religious Broadcasters, he takes the position that using mass broadcasting to save souls and spread the good news is a religious commission. This view differs considerably from the page-one headline in the May 19, 1978, *Wall Street Journal,* which blared, "Religious Broadcasting Becomes Big Business." Other observers have expressed their thoughts about the electric church in periodicals such as *Christianity and Crisis* and *The Christian Century,* as well as in more popular magazines such as *Newsweek, Harpers, Atlantic Monthly, T.V. Guide, Saturday Review, Penthouse,* and *Time.* There has, however, been a dearth of publications from the social-science community. This means that it is highly likely that no systematic empirical data on the electric church exist and that there is no discussion of theoretical frameworks. This study is intended as a first step in filling that gap.

But what have social scientists learned about the electric church? The first forum on the subject, the Consultation on the Electronic Church, was convened by William Fore of the National Council of Churches of Christ in February 1980. The meeting drew more than two hundred people—sociologists, psychologists, educators, and broadcasters, to mention a few. It was in one of the forum sessions that Hadden proposed a model to explain the growth of the electric church.

Hadden's definition of the electronic church encompasses all electronic communication that is generally perceived by senders and receivers alike as religious in intent and content (1980b:4). By defining the electronic church in this fashion, Hadden manages to avoid "pejorative connotations" while incorporating a wide variety of religious communications other than broadcasting—recordings of sermons as well as high speed computers and the word processing machines that permit television and radio broadcasters to identify and target 'personalized' communications to select audiences" (1980b:5).

Hadden believes that we cannot account for the "growth and development of the electronic church" or understand its "significance and potential" without first acknowledging its place in what he calls the "third major communications revolution" (Hadden, 1980b:5). This revolution produced the "feedback loops which permit direct communication between those who utilize the air waves and their audiences. To the novice and the naive, this communication appears highly personal" (Hadden, 1980b:7). Like the development of many business and volunteer organizations that depend heavily on such innovations, the electric church is partly an outgrowth of our own technological savvy. Together with two other factors, "control by evangelical Christians" and the "drift of American culture toward conservatism," technological developments provide us, in large measure with "a model which can explain (1) *how* the electronic church developed, (2) *who* largely controls it, and (3) *why* it has been so phenomenally successful during this past decade" (Hadden, 1980b:8).

Not only is there an affinity between the proponents of the electric church and God-given technology, but, as Hadden points out, technology and "proselytization" are congruent (1980b:9). Television is not suited for complex ideas, but it is ideal for transmitting plain and easily understood messages. While these observations may indeed provide a useful empirical orientation by which to identify major factors affecting the growth and development of the electric church, we still do not have a sociological theory for understanding the "significance and potential" of its development. For this, we need to turn to another arena of study—mass communications.

Mass-communications research is, according to Merton (1957), the American version of the sociology of knowledge. "The American version is primarily concerned with public opinion, with mass beliefs, with what has come to be called 'popular culture' " (1957:441). Among the suggested categories of analysis in Merton's paradigm for the sociology of knowledge is his answer to the question "Where is the existential basis for mental production located?" Merton further suggests that social bases to examine in this connection are

> occupational role, mode of production, group structures (university, bureaucracy, academies, sects, political parties, "historical situation," interests, society, ethnic affiliation, social mobility, power structure, social processes (competition, conflict, etc.).
>
> Cultural bases: values, ethos, climate of opinion, Volksgeist, Zeitgeist, type of culture, culture mentality, Weltanschauungen, etc. (1957:460)

Since the electric church, as Hadden defines it, includes all varieties of technological components, it may be argued that the electric church is also a phenomenon of popular culture. Popular inspirational religion appears in the "flood of books, pamphlets, magazines, and newspapers' as well as in television and radio (Schneider and Dornbusch, 1958). As such, it fits comfortably into Merton's paradigm. However, while we acknowledge our debt to the sociology of knowledge for a large-scale interpretive framework, we are still without a middle-level theory to connect this abstract paradigm to the systematic study of television programs. Two previous studies are relevant here. The first is *The Television-Radio Audience and Religion* by Parker, Barry, and Smythe (1955), an examination of the religious audience in New Haven, Connecticut, which used content analysis to describe the programs. The second study, *Popular Religion* by Schneider and Dornbusch (1958), looked at forty-six best sellers of inspirational religious literature published between 1875 and 1955. Both of these studies used content analysis to understand religious phenomena in popular culture.

To find a rigorous and systematic utilization of content analysis with a theoretical basis, we have to turn to the sociology of communications. For instance, Gerbner and Gross approach content analysis through message-system analysis of television programs (1975:2). The assumption is that television messages serve to enculturate viewers and that the researcher's role is to study the "symbolic environment." The researchers hold that

> Common rituals and mythologies are agencies of symbolic socialization and control. They demonstrate how society works by dramatizing its norms and values. They are also part of a general system of messages which cultivates prevailing outlooks (which is why we call it culture) and regulates social relationships. This system of messages, and their story-telling functions, make people perceive as real and normal and right that which fits the established social order. (1975:1)

Religion and Television was a research study commissioned by an "ad hoc committee of religious leaders representing evangelical, mainline, protestant, ecumenical, Roman Catholic, and 'electronic church' religious groups" (Gerbner et al., 1984:15). Its purpose was to study the content of 101 religious television programs and their effect on viewers. Here, the enculturation model was used to compare viewers of religious television and viewers of general television. This study did not focus on either popular religion or the electric church.

In another attempt to answer some basic questions about the electric church, Liebert offered a "psychological perspective on what is going on in the war over a new religious and cultural phenomenon, the Electronic Church" (Liebert, 1980:1). Liebert is among those who view the "war" as being between fundamentalism and liberalism. These observers maintain that it is the more encompassing scope or domain of the electric church that separates it from the traditional church. The electric church provides "news, sports, variety entertainment and, most significantly, political commentary along with its religious message and solicitation of contributions. (No one who is merely trying to make money would do so.)" (1980:13). According to Liebert, using technology is psychological engineering designed to manipulate the viewer. It falls far short of providing the emotional or spiritual requisites of religion.

> One can be justifiably concerned about the special interaction that exists between the broadcast medium and the fundamentalist message. . . . the medium and the message work together to create leaders of electronic denominations whose principle characteris-

tics must be their personality and showmanship. When such an individual emerges, he is hard to dispose but easy to imitate, and this climate of competition lends great viability (as well as great authoritarianism) to the Electronic Church. New denominations are spawned not as a result of theological differences, but as a result of personal grievances and personal ambitions. (1980:19)

Liebert's assessment is gloomy for mainline churches. He envisions television ministries as

. . . setting up local community centers, with an absolute philosophic and economic tie to the denomination's charismatic leader. These centers will offer media services to congregant members via a big screen, in grandly decorated halls that will sing with fastpaced visual and sound effects built on the most advanced electronic technology. The electronic church got its start in broadcasting, but it is not merely airwave religion. (1980:13)

Speaking before the forum on the electric church, Hadden also raised four critical issues which he thought warranted systematic empirical investigations by social scientists.

1. *"The electronic church succeeds at the expense of the local congregation"* (1980:19). Are nationally televised religious programs in competition with local churches for the same members and financial support, or do these programs supplement local churches? Hadden suggests that empirical research into this question be done "under the aegis of an advisory commission with representatives from the National Religious Broadcasters, the National Council of Churches, and the U.S. Catholic Conference" (1980:20).

2. *"The electronic church is part of a broader effect to reshape American culture"* (1980:20). Although Hadden is convinced that this assertion is true, he does not believe that the First Amendment will be thrown out or that a theocratic dictatorship will be established in the United States. He does anticipate that the electronic church will have a "significant impact on the political scene" (1980:21). Television, generally, in his opinion, will become part of a power base with which to manipulate culture and politics.

3. *"The electronic church is immoral"* (1980:22). Here, Hadden addresses a common perception about the "methods" and "motives" of the electronic church, cautioning that such criticisms are not only

premature but also likely to divert attention from "real problems" (1980:24).

4. *"Television itself is harmful to our health"* (1980:23). This is a criticism of the medium and its effects on individuals and society. Hadden warns "that television and its many technological and social by-products are altering consciousness to the detriment of individuals and society as well" (1980:24). Consequently, the effect of television is another area ripe for research.

Hadden himself, with Swann, addressed these issues a year later in *Prime Time Preachers: The Rising Power of Televangelism* (1981). This was the first comprehensive and descriptive analysis of the electronic church. Hadden is schooled in the sociology of religion and held the chair of sociology at the University of Virginia. Swann is an ordained Presbyterian minister and a Doctor of Sacred Theology. He calls himself a professional Christian "communicator" (Hadden and Swann, 1981:xviii). *Prime Time Preachers* covers audience characteristics, program themes, and the business aspects of the electronic church.

In their study, Hadden and Swann examined audience characteristics to explore competition between teleministries and local churches. Using Arbitron data for February 1980, they found that the audience of the electric church is primarily based in the Bible Belt and made up largely of females over fifty years of age (1981:61). This evidence lends some credence to the claim that the electric church has a different constituency than do mainline churches. This generalization has been supported by subsequent studies that depict the viewers as older, less-educated, lower-income (and, according to Gerbner, nonwhite) females. They are also more likely to be members of evangelical-fundamentalist churches. There are, nonetheless, exceptions. The Gerbner study noted that some prominent teleministries drew viewers who were younger, white, and better educated (1984:70). Recent Nielsen data confirm Hadden and Swann's original description of the audience as mostly female, but also indicate that a larger proportion of men watch than had been recognized, and younger men are attracted to Jerry Falwell and the "700 Club." In fact, children make up 30 percent of Jerry Falwell's audience. Women over 55 still compose the largest proportion of viewers, but there are larger proportions of women in the 25–54 age category watching religious television.

Stacey and Shupe's study of the electric church audience, conducted in the Dallas–Fort Worth Metroplex, found that among television viewers "the more active a person is in face-to-face church activity the more likely the person will view religious programming and/or support it" (1982:297). This was supported in the Gerbner (1984) study and is consistent with Hadden and Swann's description of the audience.

The question of audience size is the most contentious. This information has come in three phases (Hadden, 1985). In the first period were the claims made by Armstrong of 130 million viewers. In the second period were the conflicting empirical findings based on Arbitron, Nielsen, and Gallup data. And in the third period new measurements used by Nielsen for CBN revealed a larger audience base than any of the previous studies. A brief review of these findings follows.

Hadden and Swann concluded that audience estimates by evangelicals are exaggerated. Arbitron data from 1980 estimated the number of viewers for sixty-six syndicated programs to be 20.5 million (1981:50). Jerry Falwell alone, however, has claimed an audience of fifty million viewers. Arbitron audience estimates are for commercial televison stations only; they do not include accurate samples of cable viewers. Consequently, since much of the expansion of religious television has been on cable networks, its figures could be underestimates. Regardless of this problem, the evidence is plain that the most rapid audience growth occurred between 1970 and 1975, when "combined audiences more than doubled from just under 10 million to 21 million" (Hadden and Swann, 1981:55). After that, the Arbitron figures show that total audience size declined, in spite of the fact that the number of syndicated devotional programs increased (Hadden and Swann, 1981).

A different and contradictory picture emerges from the Annenberg/ Gallup research. As mentioned previously, the Annenberg team estimated the number of religious television viewers was "13.3 million, or 6.2 percent of the estimated total number of persons in television households" (Gerbner, et al., 1984:3). Gallup took a representative survey of viewers and nonviewers and found that "approximately one in three adults had watched religious television in the past 30 days" (Gerbner et al., vol 2, 1984:3). The contradictions in these estimates are never discussed in the report; estimates of cable audiences are not included in either study. These contradictory estimates of audience size have confused our perception of the electric church. Critics hoping to prove that it is an unimportant phenomenon, and proponents hoping to validate its success have used the differing estimates for their own ends.

The Nielsen study for CBN brings us to the third period. This market research was undertaken by CBN for use in program planning and development. The findings supported the Gallup evidence, by showing that "40 percent of the 84.9 million TV households in America watched one of the top ten religious programs at least once during February 1985. The Gallup surveys have found that between 32 and 43 percent of all adults recalled watching a religious program in the past month" (Clark and Virts, 1985:22). These new figures indicate that the electric church is a national phenomenon as its proponents have claimed, and as the teleministries illustrate for us.

Whether the religious audience is declining, is expanding, or has stabilized, is particularly relevant for arguments concerning continued competition between the electric church and local churches. If indeed the audience for these programs is finite, then religious broadcasters will eventually compete among themselves and with local churches for support, thereby making the "conflict" more intense. Partly in response to this audience dilemma, religious broadcasters are trying to attract more cable viewers by "religious broadcasting" of a more general nature, such as Pat Robertson's soap opera, news, religious music, and so forth. It is fair to say that audience size and composition is a major concern to religious broadcasters and that they take the results of their market research and analysis very seriously. It is not unusual for larger organizations to retain the services of commercial market research firms to keep tabs on their audience.

Hadden and Swann's main concern, however, is not audience size or characteristics but the connection between the electric church and the New Christian Right:

> The real importance of the Moral Majority and other New Christian Right organizations is not in what they accomplished during the 1980 elections, but in the *potential* they represent as a burgeoning social movement.... First, there is much restlessness and discontent in America today, and much of it is mobilizable in the name of Christian virtue. The number of evangelicals in America is large—very large, second, every important social movement since the advent of television has been developed through mass communications.... The third factor that makes the potential of the New Christian Right so awesome is that its leaders have mastered the use of ancillary technology of television ... the foundation of which is direct mail targeted to audiences likely to be sympathetic to a cause. (1981:165–66)

Hadden and Swann regard the electric church as a counter-

counterculture of the Right, intent upon restoring morality, dignity to the family, and the fear of God and of Jesus' Second Coming.

Stacey and Shupe take a different stance. They conclude that the electric church "preaches to the converted who are already predisposed, or self-selected, to seek out its messages. These are persons who are members of fundamentalist congregations and/or persons with highly orthodox religious beliefs" (1982:299). They continue:

> Our findings indicate an even more limited support base within the electronic church's audience for morally directed political or public policy activities. . . . The electronic church phenomenon is not likely to fade from the American scene, particularly given mainline denominations' past participation in it and their own ambitious plans for expansion of broadcast/production facilities. However, the *evangelical* electronic church, which is the real source of the controversy, has a select and relatively modest-sized clientele, and the likelihood of a significant political movement arising out of it remains small. (1982:302)

Thus, there are two ways of looking at the role of the electric church in the development of the New Christian Right. Hadden and Swann are certain that television is a source of active and influential power for the Right. Although Stacey and Shupe's question concerns the correlates of support, that is, audience, their study implies that television reinforces existing beliefs and attitudes. As the recent Nielsen study for CBN has revealed, the electric church audience is much larger than any of these authors believed. But what is more significant is that audience size is one measure of success and only one aspect of social movement mobilization. The function of the audience and the role of the electric church in the development of the New Christian Right remains to be more systematically explored.

PART II

THE EMERGENCE OF URBAN REVIVALISM

3

THE SEEDS OF THE
ELECTRIC CHURCH

DURING THE NINETEENTH CENTURY, Protestant evangelical revivals of religion developed distinctive patterns of organization, complete with specialized roles, routinized traditions, and rituals of conversion as well as distinctive beliefs and religious values. For these reasons, we refer to "urban revivalism" as a distinct social institution, separated and sufficiently differentiated from the main institution of Protestantism to develop its own audiences, its own organizations, and its own place within American popular culture and religion.* But what is a social institution? And, specifically, what does it mean to say that a social institution is undergoing a process of rationalization and routinization?

There are many different approaches to the concept of a social institution insofar as the concept serves as a basic unit of analysis in sociology. A review of these approaches would be a digression here. There are, however, common components which, according to most sociologists, constitute the core of a working definition.

"Social institution" as used in this study owes much to Parsons' semi-

---

*The work of Ahlstrom (1972) provides a comprehensive religious history of America. Basic materials on revivalism may be found in Findlay (1969), McLoughlin (1959), and Weisberger (1958).

nal interpretation of Weber and Durkheim found in *The Structure of Social Action* (1949) and *The Social System* (1951). To Parsons, an institution is "a complex of institutionalized role integrates which is of strategic structural significance in the social system. . . . Roles develop or are institutionalized by internalized cultural values and norms" (1951:39). An institution "denotes an aspect of social life in which distinctive value-orientations and interests, centering upon large and important social concerns (e.g., education, marriage, property) generate or are accompanied by distinctive modes of social interaction" (Parsons, 1951). Social institutions are organized around major social spheres or concerns. Parsons identified six spheres: family and kinship, education, economics, politics, culture, and stratification. These spheres, or social cores, are found in all societies and, as such, constitute a regulative framework for social organization. According to Eisenstadt, "institutions or patterns of institutionalization can be defined here as regulative principles which organize most of the activities of individuals in a society into definite organizational patterns from the point of view of some of the perennial, basic problems of any society or ordered social life" (1968:410).

Religious institutions are part of the cultural sphere, transmitting beliefs and values that preserve and regulate activities in their domain and contribute to the overall stability of the social system (Parsons, 1951). Institutions, or partial institutions, conceptualized in this manner, are units of analysis suitable for a variety of comparative uses. For the analysis of social institutions, we shall follow Weber, who compared historical institutions and ultimately developed ideal types with which to compare and analyze religious and economic institutions (Eisenstadt, 1968; Weber, 1958).

A social institution comprises social roles and their related statuses as held by the people in the institution, together with the norms of behavior, values, and beliefs held by these people. Associated with these roles are techniques, rituals, and social activities which develop and become associated with ongoing institutional goals. Moberg (1962) studied American organized religion in *The Church as a Social Institution*. Included in Moberg's definition of religious institutions were "all organizations which directly seek to kindle, renew, and guide the religious life of people. It includes the roles and statuses of the persons in such groups, their ideological values, goals, and group-related activities, and all social structures and processes related to religious worship,

prayer, associated and other activities in ecclesiastical organizations"
(1962:1).

In this sense, urban revivalism is a social institution, with the specific
goal of saving sinners and offering salvation. This is its primary sphere
of religious activity. The role of the revivalist is focal to the institution,
and, therefore, his ethos (values, beliefs, and norms of behavior) determines the appropriate techniques, rituals, and messages used to meet
institutional objectives (Stinchcombe, 1978).

What accounts for institutional development, both initial and
ongoing? To answer this, we may use Weber's theory of rationalization
as an explanatory framework, which, when linked to comments by
Stinchcombe (1978), joins the concepts of rationalization and institutions: "The causal forces that make systematic social change go are
people figuring out what to do." The locus of social change, Stinchcombe continues, is the "cognitive content of people's minds." From
this it follows that "what we have to study to understand history is how
structural forces cause people to change their notions of what kind of
situation they are in, and to sustain those new notions sufficiently long
to build them into institutions that in turn sustain them" (1978:117).

Weber's Process of Rationalization

Rationalization is both a process and a theory of history (Weber,
1958:78). As a process, rationalization should be distinguished from
rationality. Rationality refers to those calculated and observable actions
used to achieve selected goals (Weber, 1958:153). Rationalization refers
to "the process by which explicit, abstract, intellectually calculable rules
and procedures are increasingly substituted for sentiment, tradition,
and rule of thumb in all spheres of activity" (Weber, 1970:26).

Rationalization, Weber argues, developed from the Puritan idea of
calling, which required the individual to demonstrate "a specific type of
conduct" motivated by the individual's need to supervise "his own state
of grace." This ascetic conduct meant a rational planning of the whole of
one's life in accordance with God's will (Weber, 1958:153). According
to Weber, "this rationalization of conduct within this world, but for the
sake of the world beyond, was the consequence of the concept of
calling of ascetic Protestantism" (1958:154).

Although the Weberian hypothesis posits that rationalization origi-
nates in the religious idea of calling, this type of behavior is not con-

fined to ascetic Protestantism. Rather, Weber continued, it is found in other "departments of life" namely "economic life . . . scientific research . . . military training . . . law and administration. Furthermore, each of these fields may be rationalized in terms of very different ultimate values and ends, and what is rational from one point of view may well be irrational from another" (1958:26). It is also appropriate and legitimate to apply the concept to both revivalism and the electric church; as Weber specifically says in a statement which has some relevance for the electric church, "to characterize . . . differences [between institutions] from the view-point of cultural history it is necessary to know what departments are rationalized, and in what direction" (1958:26).

Economic factors undoubtedly affect the rationalization process. Weber states that "the ethical ideas of duty [based on magical and religious forces] . . . have in the past always been among the most important formative influences on conduct" (1958:27). While Weber is fully aware of these economic influences, he argues that ethos, or the broad gestalt of cultural values, precedes and underpins rational action. Nevertheless, economic activity is the model for rational behavior and rationalization.

Thus, economic influences may be discerned in the capitalist's calling, defined by Weber as an "impulse to acquisition, pursuit of gain, of money" (1958:17). What is critical is that profit be "rationally pursued" and that actions be "adjusted to calculations in terms of capital. . . . The important fact is always that a calculation of capital in terms of money is made, whether by modern book-keeping methods or in any other way. . . . Everything is done in terms of balances" (Weber, 1958:18). As we shall see later, Billy Sunday calculated the cost of a soul, while today's television preachers measure their effectiveness in terms of the number of regular viewers they attract.

Critical to the rationalization process is some means of calculation to evaluate action and to base future action on. These calculations in some situations are relatively imprecise and may simply be estimates. Although the precision of the measure impinges on the "degree of rationality," it is the self-conscious, reflexive appraisal of one's conduct which determines whether action is rational or not (Weber, 1958:19).

Furthermore, rationalization of an aspect of life requires a technique or means of measurement, since at the end of any transaction (or series of transactions) some calculation is necessary to determine if the value remaining is greater than the value expended. In other words, some measure of success must be available that is empirically grounded and can be used to appraise or evaluate the means-end decisions. For this reason, goals provide not only the focus for continuous, repetitive rational action but also the objective standard by which success is measured. Therefore, intrinsic to rationalization as a process is goal attainment. When rational goal-oriented actions are continued and sustained over time, roles emerge together with patterns of relationships, norms of behavior, and values to form social structures or a social institution. In the wake of rational goal-oriented behavior, one unintended consequence, to use Merton's words, is that in the actions leading to the objective goals, the use of new and effective techniques is encouraged. New technologies are ultimately adopted when they are perceived as effective ways to achieve goals. Once adopted, their attendant behavior, techniques, and attitudes tend to become stable and routine. The ongoing process of rationalization continues as the driving force of the institution, but, at the same time, some roles and their interrelationships together with norms of behavior are stabilized and organized as a social institution.

Thus, a social institution, defined in this manner, is the result of an ongoing process of rationalization. From rational, goal-oriented behaviors, roles and patterns of behavior emerge. Together with technology, these roles are major components of the social institution. In this context, technology is the method by which all work is organized to use the resources of the system (including division of labor, techniques, tools of the trade) to achieve institutional goals. Goals serve to focus action and set standards of performance. Ethos, or values and beliefs, precedes and sustains goal-oriented behaviors. Generally, then, roles, technology, and ethos are the components arranged and patterned toward effective achievement of institutional goals (Moberg, 1962; Parsons, 1951). In our history, these components created a new institution dedicated to evangelism—urban revivalism and, in its wake, the electric church.

Urban Revivalism

In order to understand the powerful new phenomenon of the electric church, one may look at the cultural tradition from which its members claim ancestry, the Protestant evangelical revivalism of the nineteenth century. Before doing so, however, we should differentiate between the concepts of revivalism, revivals of religion, and awakenings. All three are associated with the historical development of American evangelical religious tradition.

Revivalism, revivals of religion, and awakenings are patterns of popular religion that are part of America's religious and cultural heritage. The usual image they evoke is that of the revivalist preacher traveling on horseback to mass revival meetings in cities and frontier campsites throughout America. None of the terms is linked to any one denomination; nor do they have anything to do with dissenting groups or church schisms.

On closer examination, we can, however, distinguish revivalism from revivals of religion and awakenings. The latter two denote historical processes. Revivals of religion are zealous upsurgings of religious faith and overt renewals that occur within a church congregation or community. They are very much part of contemporary church practice (Michael, 1981; Moberg, 1962) and sometimes even provide viewers for the electric church (Stacey and Shupe, 1982). Religious awakenings are associated with revivals of religion. They involve widespread and prolonged periods of religious excitement. There have been several periods in American history that historians recognize as awakenings. Some religious historians even interpret awakenings as cyclic events (Ahlstrom, 1972; McLoughlin, 1978)*

Revivalism, on the other hand, is more specific, and refers to institutionalized structures and forms used during revivals of religion. As such, revivalism is a distinctly American tradition, taking its attributes and symbolic associations from the nineteenth-century environment in which it first appeared. Social structures such as revivalist preachers, meetings in tents or large tabernacles, and large groups of religious converts were all established parts of the American revivalist movement to convert sinners to a renewed Christian life. Camp-meeting-style revivalism was popular among many denominations on the Appalachian frontier of Kentucky and Tennessee (Boles, 1972; Sweet, 1948). Methodists particularly relied on such revivals to obtain converts and members for frontier churches (Sweet, 1948). The symbolic associations of camp-style revivalism—the emotionalism, the dramatic conversions, the com-

---

*McLoughlin (1978) designated four periods of awakenings in America: 1725–1750, 1795–1835, 1875–1915, and 1945–?. This scheme is not accepted by all religious historians. See Sandra Sizer, "Politics and apolitical religion: the great urban revivals of the late nineteenth century." *Church History* 48 (1979):81–98.

munal religious fervor—today remain as part of the inherited lore of American revivalism.

Urban revivalism had the same goals as camp-meeting revivalism. Both were directed toward converting the individual sinner to a renewed Christian life (Ahlstrom, 1972; McLoughlin, 1959; Weisberger, 1958). The difference was not so much in goals and setting as it was in the fact that urban revivalism consisted of a carefully orchestrated and managed set of events, financed and planned in conjunction with local churchmen.

Although the antecedents of urban revivalism can be traced to revivals of religion in colonial times (Ahlstrom, 1972; McLoughlin, 1978), the emergence of urban revivalism as a differentiated institution took place later, from approximately 1820 to 1920. This was a period of profound change and conflict in the United States. The American economy was shifting from mercantile to industrial capitalism (Hacker, 1940). There was rapid economic growth, accelerated urbanization, and the rise of specialization in business enterprises (Chandler, 1977). Major social changes followed economic ones, including the conflict over slavery and the Civil War. This was also a period of large-scale social-structural changes brought about by mass migrations from Europe and Asia into America's urban centers.

By the end of the nineteenth century, America was no longer a *Gemeinschaft* (communal society) but a *Gesellschaft* (impersonal urban society), characterized by great concentrations of wealth, economic interdependencies, and new occupational structures. One consequence of this change was the secularization of life and the diminution of religious experience and influence (Herberg, 1960). Many religious people, under these conditions, expressed anxiety about their ability to maintain their religious identity and integrity. Revivalism promised renewal and reassurance of their religious beliefs. It was with this promise that religious revivals addressed a variety of popular anxieties of the new, more secular *Gesellschaft* (Hunter, 1983; Johnson, 1978; McLoughlin, 1959; Weisberger, 1958). The career of the professional was filled with a panoply of techniques, specialized messages to convert the sinner, and organizational routines which could be used under a variety of circumstances. Many Protestant groups subscribed to a revivalist dogma, but it was especially suited for those evangelical groups who had one simple message: "Are you born-again?" If not, "repent and be saved" (Ahlstrom, 1972, Marsden, 1980; McLoughlin, 1959). In our century, Billy Graham, Oral Roberts, Rex Humbard, and Jimmy Swaggart are direct descendants of this religious tradition of urban revivalism. All these men were revivalists before they adapted their professional skills and evangelical message to television.

In addition to being part of America's religious tradition, urban revivalism and its heir, the electric church, are part of America's secular or popular culture. The social meanings attached to the institution of revivalism come, in part, from the society in which it originated. That society was characterized by urbanization, an appeal to the individual, and democratization of salvation. The interrelationship between popular culture and religious tradition lead us to a social-institution perspective rather than a sociological church-sect frame of reference. Such a historical framework accounts for a number of the characteristics of the electric church—popular, inspirational messages; popular, mass audience support; an emphasis on preaching as the primary religious ritual; and the revivalist's evangelical zeal. Similarly, we can identify some of the social structures upon which the electric church rests in popular culture and to which it sends its messages—aspiring workers and groups whose place in society is threatened by rapid changes (Gusfield, 1976; Hammond, 1979).

This institution, urban revivalism, had a clear raison être. It was in the business of saving souls by returning strayed or lapsed Christians to a renewed Christian life. This sharply focused mission facilitated the development of urban revivalism into an institution. Although there are other important aspects of urban revivalism, my analysis is restricted to showing the development of the specific roles, techniques, messages, and ethos of this institution. It traces the historical development of urban revivalism through the careers of three key revivalists who made major changes in these institutional components: Charles Grandison Finney, Dwight Moody, and Billy Sunday.

All three were responsive to the social conditions that existed at the time. They adapted business techniques of selling to their religious callings and established entrepreneurial organizations for their evangelical purposes. Moody, for example, transformed his aggressive sales ability from his secular business career directly to his sacred "business" as a revivalist, seeing no inherent contradiction in this religious application. Findlay notes that "after Moody left the market place for full-time religious work, his social and economic values remained essentially those of a conservative entrepreneur of the post–Civil War era. His interest in spreading the Gospel, a full-scale affair from the 1860's on, can also be viewed as merely a more intense version of the same concern professed by most of his business friends" (1969:88).

There were additional changes that signaled an emerging institution. Urban revivalism was detached from congregational and denominational activities and practices, and the role of professional revivalist evolved as a specialized calling or career. A professional revivalist had one major function, namely to gather converts to Christ. Other pastoral tasks were secondary or outgrowths of this mission. His organization developed from his calling rather than his being ready to serve a pre-existing congregation. Ultimately, evangelical or revivalist organizations became independent of denominational influence and administrative controls. In fact, although most revivalists remained within evangelical Protestantism, by the end of the nineteenth century they had established their own training programs, Bible schools, and community groups. These groups became a separate network, distinct from mainstream denominational organizational networks (Findlay, 1969); Marsden, 1980; McLoughlin, 1959). This is important since many of the televangelists were educated in this system, and are developing their own training programs and schools in conjunction with their television ministries.

One of the factors contributing to this differentiation of revivalism is that the career and success of the professional revivalist was based upon his personal effectiveness and his organization skills rather than on denominational career ladders. The revivalist built his own clientele and obtained his own financial resources. He deemphasized theology and dogma and instead emphasized popular inspirational religion and culture.

> Nearly all doctrinal emphases tended to be suppressed, not only by the famous spellbinders, but by the thousands upon thousands of local ministers and now-forgotten regional itinerants. Gradually a kind of unwritten consensus emerged, its cardinal articles being the infallibility of the Scriptures, the divinity of Christ, and man's duty to be converted from the ways of sin to a life guided by a pietistic code of morals. Revivalism, in other words, was a mighty engine of doctrinal destruction. "Are you saved?" became the central question of American Protestantism; and more and more it came to mean, "Have you decided to be saved?" (Ahlstrom, 1972:845)

Since his audiences were interdenominational, the revivalist's appeals often were directed to rather generalized virtues such as family and patriotism (Bellah, 1975; Herberg, 1960).

Although the motor for this institutional differentiation is a rationalization process, it is the innovative influence of the charismatic leader which accounts for the accelerated changes in the institution. Through his messages and behavior, the charismatic leader speaks to his followers, who (if they legitimize him) provide the necessary and sufficient conditions for creative or innovative social changes (Eisenstadt, 1968; Weber, 1975).

To illustrate this type of charismatic leadership and influence, we may contrast, for example, the spontaneous, mystical religious revivals of Jonathan Edwards, which occurred during the colonial period, with the pragmatic, routinized revival crusades of Charles Finney, Dwight Moody, or Billy Sunday. According to Edwards, a religious revival was sent by the Holy Spirit and was truly a sacred event. Edwards' religious experiences and beliefs influenced his behavior. The above-mentioned revivalists, on the other hand, believed in conscious, systematic planning of their behaviors to encourage religious enthusiasm. Encouraging revivals was a rational, goal-oriented process. Over a period of time, these revivals became stable and routinized religious events (Weber, 1958). And as a consequence of this rationalization process, the saving of sinners was brought into the realm of the secular. The revival was demystified, and the process was institutionalized.

4

CHARLES GRANDISON FINNEY AND THE ETHOS OF REVIVALISM

Men are not mere *instruments* in the hands of God. Truth is the instrument. The preacher is a moral agent in the work; he acts; he is not a mere passive instrument; he is voluntary in promoting the conversion of sinners.

(Charles Finney, 1960:22)

CHARLES GRANDISON FINNEY (1792–1875) WAS AN AMERICAN evangelical preacher and educator. Trained as a lawyer, he gave up practicing law shortly after a religious conversion experience to become a Presbyerian minister (1824). In 1835, Finney published *Lectures on Revivals of Religion*, which McLoughlin noted was the "classic revivalist's text" up to Billy Sunday's era. Two years later, Finney became a professor of theology at Oberlin College, a position he retained until 1875. Finney was president of Oberlin from 1851 until 1865 and continued his revival tours until his death.

Finney left a major legacy for urban revivalism, not only by the example he set with his remarkable personal skills as a revivalist, but by articulating the ethos of urban revivalism and the logical and rational justifications upon which urban revivalism rests. Finney's *Lectures* explained to clergymen how to conduct revivals, or, in other words, how to win souls—the primary calling of the revivalist. New measures, according to Finney, were more than justified. With this one argument, Finney provided the ideological justification for making revivalism a planned event instead of a mystical, spirit-filled happening. Man was going to stimulate religious enthusiasms. This was a clear shift from a fatalistic attitude to an assertive, purposeful approach.

This is analogous to the relationship Weber posited in the *Protestant Ethic and the Spirit of Capitalism*—the relationship between ethical ascetical behaviors aimed toward salvation and the unintended consequences of capital accumulation and hard work. In Finney's situation, the ethos of revivalism was a system of beliefs and values around which a religious culture organized actions and behaviors. The ethos of revivalism included all the beliefs and values expressed by Finney—in particular, the use of any means to stir religious enthusiasms.

The new measures introduced by Finney function as a technology of revivalism, if by technology we use Merrill's definition as any "bodies of skills, knowledge, and procedures for making, using, and doing useful things. They are techniques, means for accomplishing recognized purposes. But as Weber recognized . . . there are techniques for every conceivable human activity and purpose" (Merrill, 1968:576–77). Some of these new measures, as chronicled by McLoughlin, are:

> the setting aside of a period of days for "protracted meetings" during which all other regular and sacred activities ceased while churchgoers devoted themselves entirely to prayer meetings and preaching services; the use of the anxious bench or anxious seat (sometimes called the mourner's bench) to which those particularly anxious or awakened or convinced concerning their need for salvation would repair in order to be specifically exhorted by the minister at the conclusion of his sermon; the use of anxious meetings, held in the lecture room or basements of the church or in private homes, at which the revivalist and local ministers and laymen spoke personally with the anxious and tried to convert them; the frequent use of prayer meetings, sometimes lasting all night, during which individual and congregational prayers were offered both for a general outpouring of the Spirit and for the conversion of specific sinners; the practice of permitting women to offer prayer publicly in mixed or "social" prayer meetings; the employment of a dramatic, colloquial, extemporaneous, and often vituperative preaching style by the revivalist in order to impress the congregation with the necessity for complete and immediate

submission to God; itinerant preaching by revival preachers who were "filled with the Spirit" and "felt the call" to preach, whether they were ordained or not. (McLoughlin, Finney, 1960:xxxvi–xxxvii)

Finney justified the introduction of these new measures by removing the magical dimension of revivals as a mystical gift from the Holy Spirit. A revival was not

> something above the powers of nature.... [It is] *right exercise* of the powers of nature. It is just that, and nothing else. When mankind becomes religious, they are not *enabled* to put forth exertions which they were unable before to put forth. They only exert the powers they had before in a different way, and use them for the glory of God.
>
> It is not a miracle, or dependent on a miracle, in any sense. It is the purely philosophical result of the right use of the constituted means—as much so as any other effect produced by the application of means. There may be a miracle among its antecedent causes, or there may not. (Finney, 1960:13)

This view of revivals made it incumbent on the revivalist to use skills and previous learnings in such a way as to reach the goal of saving sinners. The motivation to do this work, and the legitimation, were derived from the authority of God and His ultimate ends.

> *Religion is the work of man.* It is something for man to do. It consists of obeying God. It is man's duty. It is true, God induces him to do it.
>
> A "Revival of Religion" presupposes a declension. Almost all the religion in the world has been produced by revivals. God has found it necessary to take advantage of the excitability there is in mankind, to produce powerful excitements among them, before he can lead them to obey. (Finney, 1960:9)

Not only did Finney make it incumbent on preachers to "use any means," but he also chided them for their old, unscientific approach—an approach that did not use the logic of cause and effect to promote religion (1960:14). Finney felt that "to expect to promote religion without excitements is unphilosophical and absurd" (1960:11). "Philo-

sophical" as used here, according to McLoughlin, meant "logical, rational, or scientific." It was this reasoning that led Finney to see Calvinism's
concept of election as unscientific and contrary to the "laws of the
mind" (Finney, 1960:11).

> The connection is as clear in religion as it is when the farmer sows
> his grain. There is one fact under the government of God, worth
> [*sic*] of universal notice, and of everlasting remembrance; which
> is, that the most useful and important things are most easily and
> certainly obtained by the use of appropriate means. This is
> evidently a principle in the Divine administration. Hence, all the
> *necessaries* of life are obtained with great *certainty* by the use of
> the simplest means. . . . This principle holds true in moral govern-
> ment, and as spiritual blessings are of surpassing importance, we
> should expect their attainment to be connected with *great cer-
> tainty* with the use of the appropriate means; and such we find to
> be the fact; and I fully believe that could facts be known, it would
> be found that when the appointed means have been *rightly* used,
> spiritual blessings have been obtained with greater uniformity
> than temporal ones. (1960:15)

To summarize, Finney exhorted ministers to use any means necessary to produce powerful excitements and ultimately revivals of religion. His substantive, rational argument was that these value-oriented
actions are "should's" or hypothetical imperatives derived from scientific logic as applied to the problem of religious revivals. This argument,
in other words, was an ideological frame of reference for revivalists.

Acceptance of Finney's argument that salvation is a rational process
redefines the conditions of religious conversion and constitutes a modification of certain religious ideas and beliefs. This redefinition leads to
a search for changes in world view and attitude among converts. These
changes should be observable, at least indirectly, through changes in
behaviors and actions. This is analogous to Weber's argument that certain tenets of the Protestant ethic, when applied to daily living, influenced people's behaviors and attitudes. As Weber stated in the introduction to *The Protestant Ethic and the Spirit of Capitalism*, the general
sociological problem is showing "the influence of certain religious
ideas on the development of an economic spirit, or the *ethos* of an
economic system. In this case we are dealing with the connection of the
spirit of modern economic life with the rational ethics of ascetic Prot-

estantism. Thus, we treat here only one side of the causal chain" (1958:27). Accounts of Finney's influence by Johnson (1978) and McLoughlin (1959) attest to major changes in the institution of revivalism and the people participating in this religious system. The greater part of these changes occurred in the technology of revivalism, specifically in the actions of the revivalist—how he organized his work, the resources he used, and, finally, how he measured his accomplishments. Ultimately, these changes in revivalism technology modified the religious beliefs of the participants, both the revivalist and the audiences.

Since the basic technology of revivalism was already in the hands of the revivalist, Finney elaborated on the revivalist's professional duties, providing a theory of practices, outlining appropriate training, encouraging independence of judgment, and enumerating standards of performance (Finney, 1960:186–87). All these components are associated with professional behavior (Pavalko, 1971). In this case, the professional objective was to save sinners (Findlay, 1969; Finney, 1960).

As noted previously, rather than wait for religious excitements, the individual minister was to take an active role as an agent of God, working for revivals. Since Finney acknowledged that the "agency of God carried a revival forward," the revivalist's role then was to work within God's agency as an active participant.

Although the responsibility of the church is to present the truth, Finney's *Lectures* instructed preachers that merely learning about revivals was not sufficient; they would have to apply these instructions: "I want you, as fast as you learn anything on the subject of revivals, to put it in practice, and go to work and see if you cannot promote a revival among sinners here" (Finney, 1960:22). As noted before, Finney preached that salvation was available for all individuals and that the individual was morally free to select redemption. There was no logical excuse for anyone not to accept Jesus or not to work to be a good Christian.

The special task of the "wise minister," Finney concluded, is to use any means to stir up excitement and generate the conditions by which sinners are converted. These techniques, or *"any means,"* were intended to kindle interest and enthusiasm for Jesus among sinners. Only after this happened did the real sales pitch begin. This same strategy is used today by some television preachers. When fundraising on the air, they offer potential contributors incentives such as jewelry, records, or tapes. But the "sales" strategy only begins after the viewer contacts the teleminister for these items.

Finney's preaching style relied on sales strategy and the use of plain talk to appeal to audiences. His argument was as structured as a lawyer's brief (and influenced, most likely, by his early training in law). If one begins with the truth from the law, the argument follows from that. Similarly, in Finney's preaching and *Lectures*, the Bible is the source of law and the foundation upon which the homily is structured. Thus, Finney embedded the legacy of biblical literalism into the revivalists' preaching style, a tradition that continues today among evangelical-fundamentalist preachers. Finney favored the direct biblical words rather than sophisticated theological doctrines, just as he favored the grammar and rhetoric of plain people. This practice, which combined emotion and intellect into structure and persuasion, is part of our popular religion heritage (White, 1972).

This style of preaching using "plain talk" represented a value change in religious voluntarism, the belief in the individual's free will to choose salvation. As it was a more popular appeal, the language was more forgiving and less judgmental, since it carried with it different assumptions regarding the inherent nature of man. No longer assumed to be born in sin and unchangeable, man could now be improved.

With the new role and the change in values came a shift in the minister's responsibility. Now, he persuaded or assisted sinners to become born-again. In this subtle change in responsibility, the minister acquired influence and control over the individual's salvation, which previously had rested only with God. Thus, the work and social relationships of the revivalist preacher were changed. The preacher now functioned as gatekeeper in the heavenly hierarchy. He became God's subcontractor, using in a new way the tools of the trade: a Bible, a hymnal, and new techniques to excite religious fervor.

Measures of Success

The "conversion experience as the mark of a true Christian" (Ahlstrom, 1972:844) was a distinguishing quality of American evangelical Protestantism. The purpose of the revival was to renew piety in the individual, to commit the individual to a conversion experience by some declaration and acceptance of Christ. This way, salvation was assured.

It was Finney who instituted "the saving of souls" as the preacher-revivalist's organizing principle and who made the conversion of sinners into a measure by which all means and ministers were to be judged. "The end of the ministry is the salvation of the soul" (Finney, 1960:176). Finney not only scorned denominational dogma, but he also rejected the traditional training and education of ministers. Instead he argued that the preachers who are best educated are those "who win the most souls" (McLoughlin in Finney, 1960:xxxiv). "Make it an object of *constant study and of daily reflection and prayer*, to learn to deal with sinners, so as to promote their conversion. It is a great business on earth of every Christian, to save souls. People often complain that they do not know how to take hold of this matter. Why the reason is plain enough; they have never studied it" (Finney, 1960:172).

Finney rejected contemporary signs of ministerial success, which, traditionally, was measured in terms of denominational positions and social status. Instead, he substituted his own measures of success and wisdom. In the chapter entitled "A wise minister will be successful," he links ministerial success with wisdom "in the discharge of his office. . . . He that winneth souls is wise," but, "he is the more wise, by how much the greater is the number of sinners that he saves" (Finney, 1960:183). Finney compares the successful minister with the skilled physician who is judged on the "uniformity of his success in overcoming disease, the variety of diseases he can manage, and the number of cases in which he is successful in saving his patients. The most skillful saves the most. This is common sense. It is truth. And it is just as true in regard to success in saving souls, and true in just the same sense" (1960:185).

Finney's argument appeals to common sense and to pragmatic outcomes. Obviously, these arguments are not for the members of established and already high-status churches, but for those individuals concerned with acquiring a place in society (Johnson, 1978). The argument also has an anti-intellectual vein because, among other connotations, Finney judges ministers by their results rather than by the niceties of rhetoric and argument. Anti-intellectualism is a peculiarly American trait. This anti-intellectualism, a strong characteristic of modern fundamentalism, derives in part from Finney's pragmatism (Hofstadter, 1970; Marsden, 1970).

A minister may be *very learned and not wise*. There are many ministers possessed of great learning; they understand all the sciences, physical, moral, and theological; they may know the dead languages, and possess all learning, and yet not be *wise*, in

relation to the great end about which they are chiefly employed.
Facts clearly demonstrate this. "He that *winneth souls* is wise."
(Finney, 1960:185)

Finney's technology, to recapitulate, is both specific and completely
justified by the logic of the means-end analysis. He urges the wise
minister to use measures which "get the attention of the people to the
gospel" (Finney, 1960:181). These measures must be "wisely calculated" for their end. Finney explains that "the object is to get up an
excitement, and bring people out. They know that unless there is an
excitement it is in vain to push their end. I do not mean to say that their
measures are pious, or right, but only that they are wise, in the sense
that they are the appropriate application of means to the end"
(1960:181). Finney's contributions to revivalism were an ethos, a clearly
articulated rationale, and a specified technology for the systematic application of these principles. It is interesting to note that the ethos of
revivalism brought critical reactions for Finney's contemporary churchmen which echo many of the same criticisms and underlying value
conflicts aroused by the electric church. In fact, it can well be argued
that Finney's new measures are the origin of today's schism between
televangelists and mainstream churchmen. A brief look at some of these
controversies will illustrate this point.

Finney's new measures were criticized on a variety of grounds. For
one, "these measures had been used by 'rude camp meeting exhorters'
or 'the fanatics of the first Great Awakening'; their use in a Presbyterian
Church 'in combination with a false theology and a fanatical spirit' was
roundly deplored" (McLoughlin, in Finney, 1960:xxxvi). Another criticism was that the need for constant "novelty and excitement" could lead
to abuses and excesses by the revivalist (McLoughlin in Finney,
1960:xxxvii). The emotional style of preaching and the offer of easy
grace were also condemned. When Finney introduced a God of Love in
place of a God of Wrath and the sinner had merely to repent, the
austere consequences of election were removed (McLoughlin, in Finney, 1960:xiv).

Ostensibly, these criticisms were directed at Finney and his revivalistic practices. However, these criticisms actually reveal deep doctrinal
and value conflicts. Finney's "morally free" sinner and his rejection of
Calvinist predetermination profoundly altered the relationships between minister and church member and minister and church. In the
past, the authority of the pastor over members of the church had been

retained in part through fear of God and eternal damnation. The revivalist's persuasive power over members was fear of damnation and promise of redemption. Instead of instilling a fear of punishment, the revivalist introduced a technique of persuasion based on a dialectic of fear and hope, both powerful tools in motivating sinners to convert. Inasmuch as sinners were accountable for their own redemption (by converting), they were less dependent on the minister for signs of grace. While the minister now served as facilitator of salvation, his direct control over the church members was diminished. This in effect, democratized salvation (McLoughlin, in Finney 1960).

Concomitant changes occurred in the authority of the church as an institution over the minister and his congregation. Once responsibility and control of salvation shifted to the individual, the role and influence of church policy was reduced. Finney, in fact, left the church (as an institution) and established an autonomous ministry (McLoughlin, 1959). For Finney the revivalist, the sacred wisdom held by the educated and ordained clergy became irrelevant, and, as noted before, he openly scorned these clergymen and their uselessness in revivals (Finney, 1960:284).

Another outgrowth of Finney's innovations was the emphasis on individual morality and active evangelism. Breaking with traditional religious orientations of acceptance of predetermination, the individual as a morally free agent was no longer beholden to church elders or to clergy for his or her redemption. At the same time, the individual could exercise control over the world by supporting evangelicalism. The belief was that if all sinners converted, social malaise would disappear, since all Christians converts are morally responsible.

In 1830, Finney offered the people in Rochester, New York, the opportunity to convert the world, to "bring on the millennium in three months"* (Johnson, 1978:4), through a transformation of individual and of society. Johnson describes the appeal as follows: "God has made man a moral free agent, evil was the product not of innate depravity but of choices made by selfish men and women. Sin and disorder would disappear when they chose good over evil and convinced others to do the same" (Johnson, 1978:4). These religious appeals found more receptive listeners in segments of society that the austere and fatalistic

---

*Finney accepted the postmillennialist position, an optimistic belief that a thousand-year reign of peace and justice was imminent. After this period, Christ would return.

Calvinistic tenets did not attract. In fact, a criticism of Finney was that his emotionalism attracted lower elements in society. Indeed, the democratization of salvation appealed to those individuals previously unacceptable as church members—shopkeepers, new migrants to the city, and the like (Johnson, 1978). They had the power to choose good over evil; they had the power to choose to be saved.

Televangelists are criticized today for their emotionalism, their fraudulent theology, and their flamboyant programs. All of these accusations are reminiscent of the charges against Finney and his style of religiosity. The underlying schism between revivalist and churchmen came into the open when Finney withdrew his Broadway tabernacle in New York City from the presbytery and established a congregational form of governance for it. This parallels the situation between the independent organizations of the televangelists and mainstream religious organizations that are part of larger denominations.

5

DWIGHT MOODY AND THE ORGANIZATION OF URBAN REVIVALISM

"I look upon this world as a wrecked vessel," he said. "God has given me a lifeboat and said to me, 'Moody, save all you can.'"

(McLoughlin, 1968:24)

Legacy of Dwight Moody

WHILE FINNEY PROFOUNDLY ALTERED the ethos and preaching of revivalism, about thirty years later, Dwight Moody (1837–1899) rationalized and routinized the organization of revivalism and some of its rituals.

Moody's career spanned the period from the Civil War to the end of the nineteeth century, a period characterized by rapid economic changes. During this time, the economy changed from a market mechanism to a business-enterprise mechanism, and, as Chandler (1977) characterized this change in economic structure, the visible hand of management replaced the invisible hand of the market. In the market economy, the traditional "business form was a single-unit business enterprise," usually operating a single economic function or single product (Chandler, 1977:3). By comparison, the modern business enterprise is distinguished by two characteristics. "It has many distinct operating units, and it is managed by a hierarchy of salaried executives" (Chandler, 1977:1). The haberdashery store, for example, was transformed into a department store. Moody transformed Finney's entrepreneurial revivalism into a business-enterprise type of religion—urban revivalism. Such an organizational change made it possible to reach increased numbers of people and, in effect, to mass-produce salvation.

This transformation in the structure of revivalism occurred during the same period that the United States was changing from a small-town, agrarian society to a large urban, industrial society. The development of Moody's career exemplifies the parallel changes in the wider society. Moody was born to a well-established family in Northfield, Massachusetts. As a young man, he moved to Boston and worked as a shoe salesman. In 1856, Moody left Boston for Chicago, where he continued to work in the boot and shoe trade. He learned all aspects of successful management—aggressive salesmanship, financial management, collection of debts, profitable investing, and the hard work associated with successful entrepreneurship and empire building (Findlay, 1969:62). But in 1860, after becoming a trusted manager for his employers, he left the shoe business to begin full-time work as an evangelist (McLoughlin, 1959).

Moody's early association with religion, it is important to note, began with the Boston Young Men's Christian Association (YMCA), an organization founded only two years before he arrived from Northfield. The YMCA was "organized by young businessmen, attached specifically to no single denomination or local church, dispensing even with the familiar institutional apparatus and physical plant of a church in favor of "meeting rooms" in the business district. The YMCA blended perfectly into the commercial milieu of the cities," (Findlay, 1969:47). Moody's evangelical orientation began in Boston at the Mount Vernon Church, a relatively new church organized "as a revival church" in the early 1840s. His association with this church brought him to conversion and finally full church membership (Findlay, 1969:49–53).

In Chicago, Moody continued his evangelical activities at the Plymouth Congregational Church. Around 1859, he also worked in the YMCA as chairman of the "Committee to Visit Sick Members of the Association and Strangers." These two affiliations placed Moody in the mainstream of the evangelical Protestantism of the 1850s (Findlay, 1969:63). In 1860, he turned to evangelism as a full-time profession, thereby ending his promising business career and transferring his finely honed business skills to his new career as a revivalist.

Moody's association with nondenominational evangelism continued throughout the rest of his life. The Sabbath School, later a church, which he founded in Chicago, today remains an independent congregation. Like his personal religion, Moody's evangelical career developed independently of mainstream church work. As a professional religionist, Moody reinforced Finney's revivalism in several ways. First, he showed a genuine antagonism to denominationalism and to institutionalized religious preaching and practice. Second, Moody's self-taught and pragmatic evangelism closely followed Finney's. And third, Moody's nondenominational start encouraged his identification with popular rituals and traditions rather than with elite sacred rituals and traditions.

In 1873, Moody went to England with his music director, Ira Sankey. By the time he returned to the United States in 1875, he was recognized as a professional revivalist (Findlay, 1969). The trip to England accomplished much for him. In addition to establishing him professionally, the experience taught him practical skills and techniques to apply in urban revival meetings. He also learned the value of working with local evangelical churches, advance publicity, preliminary prayer meetings, popular music, and a trained staff. As a result of the very successful English tour, Moody was asked to hold revivals in four American cities

Plate 1. A service by Moody and Sankey at the massive Agricultural Hall in Islington, London, showing the crowds, ushers with pointers, and the platform filled with local dignitaries and notables. Courtesy Moodyana Collection, Moody Bible Institute Library.

(McLoughlin, 1959). It was shortly after the Civil War. Moody

> found the times so fearful that he dropped the old post-millennial
> outlook of Evangelicalism for a premillennial one . . . Noting the
> increasing difficulties of American society—the dominance of the
> big cities, the problems of unassimilated Roman Catholic immi-
> grants, the rise of socialist labor agitators, the widespread corrup-
> tion in business and government, increasing immorality among
> the idle rich, increasing drunkenness and wickedness among the
> poor—all of these seemed to him proof that the day of judgment
> was approaching and that only the Second Coming of Christ could
> set the world right. (McLoughlin, 1968:24)

According to McLoughlin, Moody "was the last of the great Evangelical
revivalists capable of winning the wholehearted support of all denominations and all classes of people" (1968:25). After Moody, American evangelical theology was divided between modernism and fundamentalism, with most revivalists siding with the fundamentalists.
Moody, however, was able to remain neutral in these divisive theological conflicts (McLoughlin, 1968:25).

What did Moody contribute to the development of urban revivalism
as an institution? Moody's legacy was to continue the rationalization
process through the systematic and thorough application of business
practices and organization for large-scale urban revivalism. In other
words, Moody established a revivalism technology (Weisberger, 1958).
A brief description of Moody's revivalism technology and his message
illustrates his use of business practices.

Moody's urban evangelical meetings were actually a series of carefully planned and executed revival meetings. His preliminary work,
while designed to meet organizational needs, always served to generate
expectation and anticipation among church groups. This work included
first obtaining the support of local churches, and then, with local church
cooperation, staging a series of anticipatory events such as revival
prayer meetings, additional church services, and special fasting and
prayer days before the revival. The purpose of these events was to
generate excitement in the community. Financial support was obtained
from prominent businessmen and other pillars of society prior to a
revival. With his credibility thus assured, Moody could convince other
people and church groups to underwrite expenses. In this manner,
Moody accomplished two objectives. First, he systematically guaranteed

his own expenses. Second, he generated genuine interest and commitment, including financial sacrifice, for his endeavors (Findlay, 1969; McLoughlin, 1959).

The actual work for these preliminary activities was supervised by Moody's staff prior to his arrival in the community with Sankey. The staff worked with local volunteers to make house-to-house visits, distribute handbills, and train choirs and ushers—all the activities required for revival meetings. Every detail was planned. In New York, for example,

> young men were divided with military precision into "companies" to handle the crowds in various parts of the building. Instructions used in Philadelphia meetings specified seven categories of ushers, to be identified by colored badges worn on lapel. The "Rules for the ushers" also gave explicit instructions on how to handle seating, possible disorders, and sickness in the crowd. (Findlay, 1969:204)

Part of revivalism's new technology was the physical location of the revival meeting. Moody rented large halls in tabernacles for his meetings. If these were unavailable, his staff would sometimes actually build a new tabernacle for the crusade. When preliminary organizational matters were complete, Moody and Sankey arrived in a community that was physically and psychologically prepared for a revival of religion.

The revival itself was a structured and routinized event focused on stirring up interest and keeping the audience's attention. Moody explained his *revivalist ethos* and the conduct of evangelistic services to other revivalists at a Christian Convention in 1876:

> Now, the question we have before us is, How can these services be so conducted as to make them profitable? Well, I should say you have to conduct them to interest the people. If they go to sleep, they certainly want to be roused up, and if one method don't wake them up, try another. But I think we ought to use our *common sense,* if you will allow me the word. We talk a good deal about it, but I think it is about the least sense we have, especially in the Lord's work. If one method don't succeed, let us try another. This preaching to empty seats don't pay. If people won't come to hear us, let us go where they are. We want to preach. Go into some neighborhood and get some persons to invite you into their house, and get them into the kitchen, and preach there; but

make it a point to interest the people, and as soon as they get
interested they will follow you and fill the churches. (Moody,
1876:4)

Both Finney and Moody considered revival meetings to be rationally
planned events with the revivalist center-stage, ready to use any
appropriate means to get people interested.

What management techniques did Moody use to hold the audience's
interest? The following account describes the physical details of the
revival meetings calculated to achieve Moody's purposes:

Moody conducted the services in the central tabernacle from a
platform at the front of the auditorium. This platform usually
seated several hundred dignitaries and the choir. Prominent
clergymen and leading businessmen usually found places there.
Special invitations issued by the central planning committee entitled a person to one of these seats. The ministers who sat there

Plate 2. Ira Sankey at the organ, Northfield Auditorium; Mount Hermon Quartette at left.
Courtesy Moodyana Collection, Moody Bible Institute Library.

were visible evidence of the united support given the revival by the local churches. "Bring in the ministers," Moody said, "and they will bring in their congregations." The people on the platform also provided a focus of interest for the crowd below, who craned their necks to see just what dignitaries were present for the day. Finally, these reserved seats gave Moody and his committee something akin to patronage in the hands of the politician. They gave out tickets as favors for services rendered or hoped for, in lieu of recognition of individuals from the floor during the service, or simply to satisfy the requests of their personal friends and acquaintances.

The preachers ordinarily spoke from a railed dais either raised a foot or so above the rest of the platform or thrust out in front of it. Sankey always placed himself and his melodeon close by. The arrangement gave the revival leaders and the audience unobstructed views of each other. Newspaper reporters found desks conveniently placed for them just beneath the platform. Decoration of the barn-like structures was practically impossible, although occasionally someone attempted to string the words of familiar Bible passages along the walls. (Findlay, 1969: 206–7)

Details of program arrangement were also planned to arouse interest and retain audience participation. For example, Moody's revival meetings began with thirty minutes of congregational singing. "If we are going to have successful Gospel meetings, we have got to have a little more life in them. Life is found in singing new hymns, for instance" (Moody, 1876:4–5). The effect was to generate good spirits in the audience and unify the crowd through musical participation (Findlay, 1969:208–9).

Moody's legacy was to push urban revivalism firmly into the sphere of popular religion. He addressed mass audiences with messages that appealed to traditional and familiar aspects of American life; he emphasized individualism, the family, temperance, and personal morality. He also spoke out against radical social politics, telling his listeners that individual solutions (that is, conversions to Christian life) would ultimately solve social problems (Findlay, 1969). But Moody's message was also embedded in premillennialist urgency and anxiety. Moody believed in the imminent bodily return of Christ, who would bring destruction and the final judgment of God upon the world (Findlay, 1969:125). Thus, Moody's message combined this sense of anxiety and urgency with a basic appeal to "the simple loving truth" to persuade sinners to convert (Findlay, 1969:163).

Another aspect of Moody's legacy was his belief in biblical inerrancy. Moody accepted the Bible as the word of God, infallible and unalterable. The Bible was his basis for religious study and Christian education. This belief in biblical inerrancy had a profound influence on the development of American popular religion. For one, the precept of biblical inerrancy in the belief system of today's fundamentalists is a distinct legacy from Dwight Moody. Moody also influenced the preaching style of other revivalists by relying on biblical stories as the basic paradigm for his homilies. The use of popular interpretations of Bible stories as messages was institutionalized in revivalism, and erudite and complex doctrinal sermons were rejected. Finally, the development of Bible schools stems in part from Moody's emphasis on Bible study and on the use of the Bible as the source of God's words.

Overall, Moody's major contribution to urban revivalism was to introduce a businesslike organization into the religious sphere and to institute managerial techniques to improve the operation and effectiveness of revivals. One other legacy from Moody should be noted which, although not directly related to the institution of urban revivalism, is related to its social milieu. This legacy is the social infrastructure of Bible schools and institutes. These schools—in particular the Moody Bible Institute in Chicago—educate and train students to carry on the work of Moody and other revivalists. When fundamentalism evolved as a social movement, some of these Bible schools became part of that movement. Today, these Christian schools are major building blocks for many televangelists in their attempts to evangelize and influence the non-Christian world.

Although a man of his times, Moody continued in Finney's tradition of keeping alive the religious-cultural conflicts embedded in evangelical revivalism while, at the same time, developing a solid infrastructure of urban revivalism.

6

BILLY SUNDAY
BUSINESSMAN FOR THE LORD

Efficiency was Sunday's trademark. The organization which he evolved to get the efficient results he so confidently promised was ranked by one professor of economics among the top five most successful businesses in the country, along with the Stanford Oil Company, United States Steel, and National Cash Register.

(McLoughlin, 1955:73)

Legacy of Billy Sunday

SUNDAY (1862–1935) BEGAN HIS CAREER IN 1896, just as Dwight Moody's era was drawing to a close. By 1908, Sunday's success in mass revivalism was firmly established. Sunday had emerged from a poor and fatherless childhood to become a professional baseball player and then, after switching to evangelical work, "the last great revivalist" (Weisberger, 1958). His recognition was as a national celebrity, in sharp contrast to Moody's reputation as a man of sincere commitment and of unquestioned religiosity.

Sunday diminished the religious connotation, according to Weisberger (1958) and McLoughlin (1955), and transformed urban revivals into "professional amusements" by his showmanship and commercialism. Moreover, he not only completed the transformation of urban revivalism into a permanent institution, but he also completed the popularization of this religious institution within American culture.

51

Sunday brings us to the brink of the television era. He was the last great personality to influence revivalism without the aid of mass broadcasting. He was at the peak of his career in 1910, emphasizing large-scale entertainment and streamlining Moody's churches, schools, and missions into one single-minded revivalist "corporation." As a result, the institution of urban revivalism had the ideal organizational structure for entering mass broadcasting. It also had the additional advantage of a sharp focus, which made it easy for it to adapt to the new broadcast techniques, much in contrast to denominational organizations (McLoughlin, 1955; Weisberger, 1958).

Within this context of "professional amusements," Sunday made several contributions to urban revivalism. Like Finney and Moody, Sunday methodically calculated his efforts to stir religious enthusiams and instituted his own revivalist technology to advance his position as businessman for the Lord. Like Moody, Sunday paid strict attention to preparation and management details in order to assure the success of his campaigns. He also engaged a management staff to take care of details and make the necessary preparations for his meetings. The following account from *Modern Revivalism* describes "the Sunday Party," the organization that Sunday created to go after "sales":

> . . . a corps of more than twenty experts, each of whom specialized in some particular aspect of revivalism and to whom he delegated authority to direct that aspect of the revival's activities. He had started this organization in 1900 by hiring a chorister to conduct the choirs and sing solos. That same year his wife began to accompany him and to act as his business manager. In 1904 he hired an advance agent to pave the way for him, and to act as night watchman and custodian of the wooden tabernacles which were built for him in each city. By 1906 he found it necessary to hire a research assistant to help him in gathering material for new sermons, and then he thought it would be advantageous to employ a person who would help the churches which cooperated with him to organize Bible classes. (McLoughlin, 1959:421)

As Sunday's career developed, his organization grew to include "a soloist to assist his chorister" and then a pianist for the soloist. He had a "publicity manager to feed news stories to the press, and a private secretary. . . . Other assistants became the director of men's work, the director of businesswomen's work, the director of students' work, and the reservation secretary." In addition, Sunday had his own house-keeper and a personal masseur as part of his traveling entourage (McLoughlin, 1959:421). Such organizational details were expensive, and Sunday, like Moody before him, obtained advance guaranteed financial backing from local churchmen and businessmen. He was particularly adroit in using the churchmen's fears of divisiveness and secularization (McLoughlin, 1959:416) for his own purposes. His efforts to attract church members by popularizing religion were readily accepted; few ministers wanted to challenge him as being too expensive (Weisberger, 1958:223). As for the businessmen, Sunday built on their desires for status and recognition and on their fear of seeming sinful with their new affluence. Association with Sunday's revivals gave businessmen a legitimacy that helped them to serve as examples of respectability in the eyes of their employees.

Sunday's revivals carried Finney's principles of appropriate means to such an extreme of businesslike efficiency that the gulf between his style of scientific management of religion and the style of the defenders of revealed or transcendental faith grew large: the two styles clearly represented conflicting values and attitutes. Sunday's revivals were severely criticized for their commercialism. Sunday argued in turn, as Finney had, that his expenditures were justified by a cost/benefit analysis of the large number of people he converted to Christianity during his campaigns, going so far as to calculate the cost as $2.00 a soul (Ellis, 1917; McLoughlin, 1955; Weisberger, 1958). The extent of Sunday's activities is described as follows:

Costs rose, but so did the number of converts. Ministers found that a Sunday campaign was a steep but useful purchase, and larger and larger towns indicated a willingness to make the investment. Up to 1906 over half of the Sunday revivals were in towns with populations of fewer than two thousand five hundred. By 1908, however, he had been as far afield as Spokane, Washington. By 1910 Youngstown, Ohio, and Boulder, Colorado, had heard his voice. In 1911 he had graduated to Toledo. In 1913 he worked in Columbus, Wheeling and Wilkes-Barre. In the climactic years between 1914 and 1919 he preached in Pittsburgh, Philadelphia, Baltimore, Boston, Los Angeles, Dallas, Detroit, Washington and New York. There were nine revivals, in those years, in mammoth cities of more than half a million souls. Two hundred thousand dollars was thrown into the New York meetings, but a triumphant ninety-eight thousand "conversions" were claimed. Sunday averaged forty thousand "decisions" in his revivals of places with more than five hundred thousand residents. It was the biggest kind of "big business for the Lord." Sunday had multiplied the force of the new methods in revivalism until he constituted a religious upheaval. (Weisberger, 1958:246–47)

Charges of Sunday's commercialism were given added fuel by the revivalist's manner and life style. Offstage, Sunday lived and dressed like a wealthy man, and, in fact, he died a millionaire. He bequeathed his home in Winona Lake, Indiana, for use as a summer retreat (Michael, 1983), but no schools or bible institutes remain as memorials to his

Plate 3. Billy Sunday gesticulating as he dramatizes his message. Courtesy H. Armstrong Roberts, Inc.

evangelicalism. Compare this to Moody's life style of personal asceti-
cism, his support of the YMCA movement, and his building of three
Christian schools. Sunday's on-stage style of revivalism, which included
exaggerated and strident preaching, drew its share of criticism as well.
The following account gives ample evidence of Sunday's "dramatic
talents":

> He acted out the homely little stories and the Bible vignettes
> which had become a revivalist's stock in trade, and he gave them a
> breath-taking vigor. Sunday skipped, ran, walked, bounced, slid,
> and gyrated on the platform. He would pound the pulpit with his
> fist until nervous listeners expected to hear crunching bone. He
> would, in a rage against "the Devil," pick up the simple kitchen
> chair which stood behind the reading desk and smash it into
> kindling; once it slipped away from him and nearly brained a few
> people in the front rows. As he gesticulated and shook his head,
> drops of sweat flew from him in a fine spray. Gradually, he would
> shed his coat, then his vest, then his tie, and finally roll up his
> sleeves as he whipped back and forth, crouching, shaking his fist,
> springing, leaping and falling in an endless series of imitations.
> He would impersonate a sinner trying to reach heaven like a ball
> player sliding for home—and illustrate by running and sliding
> the length of the improvised tabernacle stage. (Weisberger,
> 1958:247)

In this account, Sunday acts out his religiosity, a technique well suited
for the visual arts, and takes revivalist preaching another step closer to
television.

Sunday also put his own mark on Moody's story-telling technique,
making the stories resemble TV minidramas. What we see today on
television (the vignettes of fast living on the "700 Club," for example) is
reminiscent of Sunday's visual storytelling. Moody relied on his ability
to relate Bible stories as if to a child, "to recite a piquant anecdote, to
inject pathos and humor into the biblical accounts he used repeatedly
in his sermons" (McLoughlin, 1959:223). Sunday, on the other hand,
relied on dramatization and on entertaining techniques to enthrall his
audience.

> Every story was a pantomime performance. Naaman the leper,
> washing himself in the Jordan to cleanse away his sores, was

reproduced with extravagent vitality by the evangelist, who would stand shivering on the bank, stub his toe on a rock, slap sand fleas, shriek with cold at the first plunge, and blow and sputter as he emerged from each healing dip. Crowds guffawed as Sunday depicted a society woman cuddling a pug dog, a staggering drunk weaving into a saloon, or a mincing preacher ordering groceries in his pulpit manner. Hurling some imprecation at a "boozer," the ex-outfielder would leap to the edge of the platform, one leg stretched out behind him, his whole taut, tense body like a javelin held in rest a few inches off the ground. Drama critics who saw the performances in the tabernacle agreed that no stage imitation of Sunday could begin to reflect the reality of him. (Weisberger, 1958:247)

Note also that besides making his preaching entertaining, Sunday applied moral lessons to contemporary characterizations; the boozer and the idle society women, were, for example, illustrative of social problems.

Sunday's preaching message also differed from that of his predecessors. Sunday's appeals were based on demagoguery, appealing to crowds with extravagant or specious arguments. He resorted to calling up the various foes of cherished values to exhort the sinners in the audience. He supported the values of "womanhood, cleanliness, God, America, hard-work" (Weisberger, 1958:249), while opposing the violators of these values. This brought audiences to climaxes of pure hatred, a shift in emphàsis from Moody's God of love.

Sunday's patriotism in the pulpit was demagoguery. At the same time, it placed him squarely in the cultural tradition of fundamentalism.

Billy Sunday . . . competed with George M. Cohan and Teddy Roosevelt for the position of most extravagant patriot. Although Sunday had little interest in the war until the United States joined it, he soon concluded that zeal for the Gospel and patriotic enthusiasm should go hand in hand. It apparently did not strain his principles (which included premillennialism and opposition to the "social gospel") to conclude in 1917 that "Christianity and Patriotism are synonymous terms and hell and traitors are synonymous." As the war effort accelerated he used the rhetoric of Christian nativism to fan the fires of anti-German furor and was famous for sermons that ended with his jumping on the pulpit waving the flag. "If you turn hell upside down," he said, "you will find 'Made in Germany' stamped on the bottom." Praying before the House of Representatives in 1918 he advised God that the Germans were a "great pack of wolfish Huns whose fangs drip with blood and gore." (Marsden, 1980:142)

How was Sunday's patriotism different from the evangelical Christian's belief in the manifest destiny of America as a sacred tenet? In Moody's era, the period following the Civil War, evangelical Christians interpreted the Civil War as a "reaffirmation of America's manifest destiny.... the war was the final stage in the national drama of self-purification and dedication in preparation for the millennium. Henceforth, to be a good Christian was to be a good patriot and vice versa" (McLoughlin, 1978:21). When Sunday combined this evangelical belief with current social issues—nativism, the Red scare, racism—into what McLoughlin calls "100% Americanism" (1978:444), a new stridency and divisiveness were injected into the evangelical Christian message. It is Sunday's black-and-white thinking which Hofstadter comments on in his analysis of American anti-intellectualism:

> A mind totally committed to the full range of the dominant popular fatuities and determined that no one shall have the right to challenge them. This type of mentality is a relatively recent synthesis of fundamentalist religion and fundamentalist Americanism, very often with a heavy overlay of severe fundamentalist morality. The one hundred percenter, who will tolerate no ambiguities, no equivocations, no reservations, and no criticism, considers his hand of committedness an evidence of toughness and masculinity. (1970:118–19)

With his harsh biblical rhetoric and his categorical patriotism, Sunday combined in his messages tensions and conflicts that were rooted in the previous century. He carried forward the anti-intellectualism traceable to Finney's scorn of the educated minister, as well as the schism between fundamentalists and modernists over questions of the infallibility of the Bible on such issues as evolution and biblical authority (Marsden, 1980).

With Sunday's influence, two extremes latent in revivalism were combined— popular entertainments and superpatriotism—to make urban revivalism a highly visible and marketable form of public religiosity (Bellah, 1980). But in the process, other precedents were set for the institution of revivalism. Sunday finished the ongoing process of taking revivalism out of denominational or institutional Protestantism and placing it in the realm of popular culture. This meant that in terms of institutional development, revivalism was a differentiated institution. Sunday drew his support and his measures of success from the business world instead of from the sacred realm. He justified his work and the expenditures with a cost-accounting rationale, not in terms of a calling or mission, as Finney and Moody had done.

Sunday described his revivals as sales campaigns for the Lord. Addressing businessmen, Sunday wrote: "I am not only a preacher, but [a] businessman; I endeavor [to] bring: 1. System-Organization; 2. Business principles; 3. Common sense into the work of the church" (McLoughlin, 1955:73). For over a decade, Sunday's voice and interpretation of evangelical work influenced evangelical churches throughout America.

Generally speaking, urban revivalism between 1820 and 1920 developed the components of an institutional system working towards a new goal—saving sinners from damnation and offering salvation to the individual. No longer was salvation predetermined, as it had been in the Calvinist tradition of election. The individual was a morally free agent, able to select salvation by accepting Jesus. The impact of this message change democratized redemption (McLoughlin, 1959). As the agent of God, the revivalist acquired enchance authority and power vis-à-vis the sinner and the saved, so that if they accepted his calling, he gained legitimacy and status. Thus, in the passing of the years, the revivalist became a professional man of God, separate and distinct from the seminary-educated clergy.

Finney's innovative contribution to revivalism through this change in conversion practices started a rationalization process which Moody and Sunday continued until the years of World War I. Moody was an exemplary revivalist whose aggressive and enthusiastic evangelical style served as a model for many revivalists. He not only exhibited a business-like approach to saving souls, but also left a legacy of educational institutions which formed the basis for twentieth-century developments. Sunday's career marked the end of one stage of development in this historical chain of revivalists. Later, significant changes or dimensions were added through the use of radio and TV. With Sunday, revivalism was standardized to such an extent that it can be compared to Taylorism, or scientific management, in the pulpit. The organization of the revival meeting, the division of labor, and the management tech-

niques perfected by Sunday and other revivalists were systematically
practiced toward the goal of gathering souls. Scientific management, as
Braverman explains, applies the "methods of science to the increasingly
complex problems of the control of labor in rapidly growing capitalist
enterprises" (1974:85). Similarly, Sunday established managerial control over his crusades and his workers in the vineyard of the Lord, and
this, Sunday argued, increased his productivity, as measured by the
number of converts he made (McLoughlin, 1955).

The Ideal Type of Urban Revivalism

By the end of Billy Sunday's career, urban revivalism was a separate and
differentiated institution, one for which it is now possible to construct
an ideal type that will serve as a basis of comparison with the electric
church. Before describing urban revivalism in more detail, however, we
briefly need to explain the concept of an ideal type.

> In his world-historical, comparative studies, Weber made use of
> bench-mark concepts, called ideal types, which deliberately sim-
> plify and exaggerate the evidence; examples are his formulation
> of the theological doctrines of Luther and Calvin, his typology of
> domination or of urban communities, and so on. . . . he saw his
> task as first the formulation of ideal types on the basis of compara-
> tive historical evidence, and then the analysis of the subject under
> investigation in terms of its deviation from, or approximation to,
> these concepts. (Bendix 1968:499)

The ideal-type urban revivalism carefully abstracts the skeletal parts in
order to see the essential shape of the institution. By baring the underlying structure, we see the essential shape and arrangments of urban
revivalism. Through this methodological technique, the clock of history
is stopped for heuristic purposes.

As discussed earlier, the main attributes of an institution are:
(1) its distinctive *ethos*, (2) the *roles* around which its social structures
develop, and (3) its *technology*, in this case the bureaucratic organization which routinizes and binds these components into an institution.
The ideal type of urban revivalism includes each of these three elements.

1. The *ethos* that distinguishes urban revivalism from denominational
religion is based on a belief that religious conversion can be stimulated

and encouraged by conscious planning. Thus, the religious experience can be rationally calculated, and any means may be used to reach people. From this, it follows that the role of the minister-revivalist is to utilize any technology which, in the final calculation, contributes to saving sinners. This ethos, once accepted, justifies and encourages, as normative practices, constructing new buildings (that is, tabernacles), employing large staffs, and using sophisticated business techniques— practices which, in the previous century, were clear departures from churchly or traditional practice to modern or goal-oriented practice (Weber, 1958).

2. The *role* of the revivalist as a preacher is central to urban revivalism. It is the revivalist who, through his actions or role enactments, translates the ethos of revivalism, first by defining the situation, then by attaching meaning to environmental cues that organize and structure his behavior. This process of symbolic interaction on the part of revivalist is built on interpretations of pertinent goal-oriented behavior, namely increasing and maximizing the number of souls converted to Christianity. Part of defining the situation also involves "naming others and naming oneself" as part of the situation—in other words, defining the roles or positions in the situation (Stryker, 1980:57). In this sense, Finney, Moody, and Sunday, through their "definitions of the situations," created the organizations and applied the ethos of revivalism.

The role of the revivalist was now an autonomous profession with self-defined missions or callings. The revivalist's training process was self-directed, often entailing rejection of a secular career, and involved trial and error as part of the learning. What worked well was used, what did not was dropped—this was the rationale for new practices, in direct rejection of traditional pastoral or ministerial practices. One aspect of this professional automomy was the necessity for revivalists to build their own organizational and financial resources, which they did with a clientele of their own. Congregationally based ministers, of course, had to engage in fundraising, too; however, the revivalists required large amounts of money to support their ongoing work, and, unlike other ministers, had no church property or other resources available to them. Instead, free-standing fundraising organizations developed by the revivalists were in large measure requisite for their survival. The revivalist's role was more akin to that of an entrepreneur than to that of a minister or churchman (Niebuhr, 1956, Scherer, 1980).

There were disadvantages of this role for both the revivalist and his constituency. The revivalist continually had to maintain and attract audiences, to demonstrate his gift or calling from God (Weber, 1958), and to recall Finney's pronouncement that "a wise minister will be successful" (Finney, 1960). The successful revivalist was rewarded and supported by his followers, based on the number of converts gathered for the Lord. Sunday, for example, released the number of converts to the newspapers after each meeting (McLoughlin, 1959).

The revivalist, with his clear task, approached his work by actively trying new techniques and styles of preaching, by appealing to the popular and commonplace, and by using psychological and organizational tricks, inspiration and communal singing, the sawdust trail up the aisle of the tabernacle to muffle the footsteps of the converted—all carefully calculated to sell the Lord. All this was done with the assistance of a paid staff and an organization. The organizational activities culminated in the revival meetings themselves, with the standardized programs and the anticipated numbers of decisions for Jesus.

3. This *technology* completed the routinization of charisma (Weber, 1958). Both the preparatory procedures and the revival meeting itself were routinized and codified. The procedures were simplified so that they could be easily learned, and the details of advance publicity, choir rehearsal, and tabernacle construction could be supervised by one staff member each. In the end, the revivalist retained control and management over his organization and the process for saving sinnners, but the technology of revivalism worked regardless of the personality of the revivalist, because the means had been institutionalized in a bureaucratic structure.

As a new free-standing institution with scientific management in the pulpit, revivalism became available to anyone with energy and entrepreneurial skills who wanted to put these institutional dimensions into a new context. This is exactly what happened. The new concept, in turn, started a modification process by changing the constellation of variables. The process of rationalization began anew when some revivalist took urban revivalism into a new medium of communication—the television industry—a new transformation began with the use of this new technology.

PART III

THE TELEVISION INDUSTRY AND RELIGIOUS BROADCASTING

7

TELEVISION
INSTITUTION FOR PROFIT

Why is there no network that rejects all programming that is amoral and majors in wholesome entertainment? Certainly not because there aren't enough people who would prefer it to the degenerate fare that is common today. The humanists see TV as a vehicle, first, to indoctrinate and second, to make money. . . .

(Tim LaHaye, 1980:157)

THE TERM *MASS COMMUNICATIONS*, although often used interchangeably with mass broadcasting, refers to all forms of mass media: television and cable television, radio, movies, magazines, and newspapers. Television and radio make up the main elements of mass broadcasting. Today television is the larger and more influential of these two media. Some of the features and characteristics of today's television are best understood from a historical perspective, while others can be explained in terms of the imperatives of the medium itself.

Before we can understand the electric church of the 1980s, we must place religious broadcasting in the larger context of the broadcast industry, and, in particular, the television industry. As one of the electric church's two parents, the television medium contributed directly to the growth and development of this new hybrid institution.

The Structures of the Television Industry

When television became a national medium, it displaced radio's twenty-five years of dominance in transmitting entertainment and news. At this time, several structural features of radio were simply imposed on the television system (Baker and Ball, 1969; DeFleur and Ball-Rokeach, 1977:63–105). Some of these features still influence program content and what we see on the screen.

Television, like the radio industry before it, is regulated by the Federal Communications Commission (FCC), which was established by the Communications Act of 1934 to "regulate broadcasting in 'the public interest, convenience and necessity.' Congress gave the FCC the power to license broadcasting stations, to assign wavelengths, and to suspend, or revoke the licenses of stations not serving the public interest." (Baker and Ball, 1969:28) This regulatory process granted a limited number of business firms the right to use the airwaves. The operations of the firms, including the content of broadcasts, were in the corporate domain, although limited by regulatory guidelines, by norms of public interest, and by cultural definitions of public taste and respectablity. The major tool of the FCC was the licensing review, which was subject to legal review as well as to pressures from the political process (Altheide and Snow, 1979; Cole and Oettinger, 1978; Cantor, 1980).

Although the FCC had the power to restrict use of the airwaves, it had no direct role in determining program content or in operating technical facilities. Its mission was to oversee an orderly use of the airwaves. Broadcasting in America is totally in the private domain and forms a segment of the communications industry that is clearly part of the marketplace. Within this context, it professes to be championing free speech and guarding free expression of ideas. This public role is different in other countries, in which mass communcations are consciously considered part of the country's cultural resources and not simply mechanisms for profit making. This difference in basic orientation has had a profound effect on the ethos of religious broadcasters (DeFleur and Ball-Rokeach, 1975, Burns, 1979; Cole and Oettinger, 1978; Cantor, 1980).

Early on, businesses recognized radio's potential as an advertising medium. The large audiences generated by radio programs enabled sponsors to sell products and services to mass markets. Not long after that, stations and networks responded with a celebrity system to attract and hold audiences for their sponsors. This practice was well established by the time television adopted the same profit-making techniques (Barnouw, 1978).

A third structural feature of American radio which was adopted by television was the standardization of program units. Fifteen-minute modules were used on the radio, and programs of fifteen, thirty, or sixty minutes, precisely on the hour, were the usual practice in the radio industry. From the start, television programs were standardized in the same manner (Baker and Ball, 1969:28; Burns, 1979).

The profit-making orientation of mass broadcasting clearly influences its programming (Goldsen, 1977; Barnouw, 1978). Access is severely restricted (both by costs and by time limitations) and therefore highly prized. The potential number of broadcasters far exceeds the capacity of the media. To a great degree, this feature gives mass broadcasting, especially television, its influence, prestige, and profitability (Owen et al., 1974; Cantor, 1980). Radio and television programs are selected to attract audiences who are potential customers for their sponsors' products. While the standardization of time segments constrains program content, it also produces convenient units for which to sell advertising (Barnouw, 1978; Gitlin, 1979). This division into units reflects the inherent rationalization of the industry. Entertainment, in the sense of any programming that will appeal to mass audiences, is the staple of a profit-oriented broadcasting industry. The only restraint on this profit objective is the FCC licensing guideline, which requires a proportion of nonentertainment programming. Nonentertainment broadcasting includes community news, health information, and educational forums along with religious programs (Cole and Oettinger, 1978).

Entertainment programs appealing to popular or mass audiences served radio advertisers well, and relatively few production changes were made to adapt them to television. Television broadcast primarily entertainment and news and often used well-known personalities. In its early days, shows were crafted by the actors and writers of the program; one might say they were hand-made as opposed to machine-made. The popular entertainments of the day—vaudeville acts, music, dramas, comedies—were either filmed or brought to a studio for transmission with little substantive alteration. The major changes for the new context consisted of tailoring the program to the time slot and adding commercial announcements (Barnouw, 1978).

Early Religious Broadcasting

Religious broadcasting goes back to the early days of radio. The first religious radio broadcast was transmitted in 1921 on KDKA in Pittsburgh, from the Calvary Episcopal Church. After that, a variety of religious organizations, including evangelicals, broadcast on radio. Some purchased their own stations. By 1925, there were "at least sixty-three stations ... owned by institutions under church influence" (Fore, 1980b:16). This proliferation of church-owned stations, however, turned out to be short-lived. By the 1930s, as the commercial market recognized the profitability of owning radio stations, religious stations all but disappeared. Although the number of church-owned stations was greatly reduced, there were still two types of air time available for religious broadcasts: sustaining air time (contributed by the station) and commercial air time (purchased by the religious organizations).

A brief digression is necessary here to explain the FCC licensing requirements that created these two categories of air time. FCC policy requires licensees to provide sustaining time so that a fixed percentage of programming is dedicated to public-interest broadcasting. "By 1929 the Commission (FCC) had ruled that religious broadcasting was a necessary program category for broadcasting in the public interest, convenience, and necessity" (quoted in Ellens, 1974:29). Therefore, when stations renewed their licenses, they had to demonstrate compliance with public-interest guidelines (Cole and Oettinger, 1978; Cantor, 1980). This "public-interest" air time was given in addition to whatever commercial time religious groups wished to buy. Around 1931, the networks and the Federal Council of Churches of Christ (FCCC) changed their policies to provide only sustaining time (Fore, 1980b:20), which was allocated by the FCCC to the major mainstream religious groups.

NBC and ABC called the practice of providing free air time through the FCCC a pragmatic move to avoid conflict and the appearance of favoritism among various religious denominations. By working with the FCCC and establishing a framework for all "cooperative Protestant broadcasting" (Ellens, 1974:28), the networks were able to shift responsibility for programming decisions to the FCCC and, through it, to the denominations themselves. In practice, a close relationship existed between NBC and the FCCC throughout the 1930s and 1940s. The FCCC was, in effect, "the major representative of religion in broadcasting" (Ellens, 1974:30). One legacy of this pattern, according to Ellens, is that religious broadcasters had to request time from the industry; the industry never felt obliged to provide religious broadcasting as part of its "community responsibility" (Ellens, 1974:30). With this pattern, later the stations easily adjusted to selling what they had once given away.

The second legacy of this NBC and ABC policy, over and above the uncertainty created by the churches' dependency on the networks for sustaining time, was the inability of independent and fundamentalist groups to buy air time from these networks. This forced these marginal religious groups, who were not part of denominational life or members of FCCC, to purchase air time on independent stations (Fore, 1980b; Ellens, 1974). This general pattern of mainliners using sustaining time and independents using commercial time still exists today in many television and radio markets.

According to Fore, broadcast policy varied among Protestant groups. "The liberal, larger, 'main-stream' Protestant denominations working through the FCCC" supported the use of sustaining time and, at the same time, were wary of diverting too many church resources for broadcast-related expenses. The smaller, marginal, and conservative groups, of which the fundamentalists were part, felt that they were being denied sustaining time, but were eager to use both radio and television to preach their evangelical message, even if they had to purchase broadcasting time (Fore, 1980b:22).

The Changing Market Environment for Religious Broadcasting

Up to the 1960s, religious broadcasting followed the pattern that had emerged in the 1930s and 1940s. Sustaining programming was used by the more mainstream Protestant groups, while commercial programming was used by the more conservative and fundamentalist groups. Independent or nonaffiliated stations broadcast the commercial programs (Bleum, 1969). According to Bleum's analysis, a national average of two and one half hours per week, per station, was devoted to religious television—sustaining and commercial, and this was broadcast on Sunday mornings (Bleum, 1969).

During the 1960s, economic and policy changes in the television industry significantly altered the broadcast situation, laying the foundation for the electric church that was to appear a few years later. One key change came from the fact that the loss of advertising revenues from tobacco and liquor commercials forced stations to find new sources of income. As a result of this economic shift, many stations became receptive to selling broadcast time to religious programmers (Goldsen, 1977; Ostrander, 1981).

The second change occurred with regard to the sale of sustaining time for religious programming. Over the years, network policies which had previously prohibited selling air time to religious broadcasters were modified. In 1949, ABC was the first network to begin selling religious broadcasting time (Ellens, 1974:31). A third and more profound change, this time in FCC regulatory policy interpretation, effectively removed for local affiliates and independents any barriers to selling religious air time. Finally, in 1960, a new FCC interpretation permitted commercial, as well as sustaining, religious programming to meet the public-interest obligations required of licensees. With this new interpretation, local stations could fulfill their licensing obligations and also generate income with one program (Lacey, 1978; Mathews, 1980). It is important to note that, by the 1960s, local affiliates of the networks had acquired greater autonomy from their national organizations, a freedom that enabled them to sell to religious sponsors without jeopardizing either their network ties or their license renewals (Lacey, 1978).

Thus, the combination of economic pressures and the removal of policy barriers created a new market environment with more time available for religious programmers. This opened the channels of access for all commercial religious programming and stimulated the entry of many religious programmers into radio and television. The increase in available time also carried with it better-quality air time at reasonable prices. This, in turn, enabled programmers to begin building a stronger audience base for future expansion (Ostrander, 1981). No longer having to confine their religious broadcasts to early Sunday mornings, independent stations sold evening time as well, including what up until then had been their "dogtime"—network prime time (Ostrander, 1981; Shoubin, 1982).

The Routinization and Packaging of Television Programs

In addition to shifting market elements, another set of changing factors contributed to the burgeoning of religious broadcasting. The television industry itself developed from the craft system to a mass-production system. Early television program production, unlike its later counterpart, was not routinized. As programming was gradually standardized, the television industry transformed into a rationalized, bureaucratic production system (Braverman, 1974).

Because the television industry was organized to meet business objectives, program selection and production were based on economic criteria, while artistic merits were virtually neglected. According to the Weberian analogy, television's spontaneity and creativity were replaced by measures of audience demographics and other elements tied to economic worth (Goldsen, 1977; Mankiewicz, 1978; Cantor, 1980).

The visible hand of management (Chandler, 1977) brought into the television production process new pressures for planning, market research, and standardization of product in order to improve market share and profitability (Weber, 1964b; Braverman, 1974). The television industry, as explained by Owen, came into the business of "producing *audiences*," which were then "sold to advertisers"; it was no longer in the business of broadcasting. Success for the industry "is measured in dimensions of people and time. The price of the product is quoted in dollars per thousand viewers per minute of commercial time" (1974:304). All parts of the industry, from station owners to program producers and performers, felt these economic incentives and pressures and incorporated these factors into their professional decisions.

In contrasting early television programs with contemporary programs, one sees the effect of this rationalization of production and program. Early television programs were live telecasts that encouraged creativity, experimentation, and the use of various styles of materials. Although the machinery of television filming was cumbersome, the resulting programs were spontaneous. Today, television technology is streamlined and versatile, with such things as mobile cameras, portapak video cameras, and instantaneous editing equipment. Despite this improved technology, program messages have been standardized to fit a limited number of patterns and variations. Part of the explanation is in the underlying rationalization process and its effects on the television industry. It is not the technology, the machinery per se, which changes the situation; it is the work process, which, in turn, is altered by the managers and owners of the networks. Braverman clearly states this point in *Labor and Monopoly Capital* when he claims that "the key element in the evolution of machinery is not its size, complexity, or speed of operation, but the manner in which its operations are controlled" (1974:188).

Applying Braverman's theory to the television production process suggests that technology, in and of itself, does not account for basic content changes (that is, standardization, etc.). Rather, the fundamental change occurs in the control of the work system. Decisions have been removed from writers, performers, and directors and given to financial and marketing staffs. Not only have these people lost most of their program influence, but they also have been deskilled. Financial managers determine the outline of marketable programs; creative staff only "fill in the blanks" of a program script (Cantor, 1980; George, 1981; Hurdle, 1981). This change signifies that value-oriented rationality—the creative elements—has been replaced with market-oriented values (Weber, 1958).

This change to market-oriented values accounts, in large measure, for the general disenchantment with network television programming among many critics of American television. There is no denial among broadcasters that rating shares, size, and audience demographics are their primary concern. The fact that the Public Broadcasting System functions to meet the public's demand for "high" culture, to use Gans' term, simply gives the commercial system more leeway to produce programs that meet the sponsors' demands for "low-culture," high-sale programming.

The Religious Television Market

Today, the basic market pattern of religious television continues to be bifurcated: sustaining air time is available for mainstream Protestantism, commercial air time for peripheral or independent Protestantism. This second category of broadcasting constitutes the electric church. This basic market pattern was laid down in the early days of radio, when "conventional" or mainstream Protestant broadcasting made up only 28 percent of the total religious output, "while the fundamentalist or 'irregular' religious broadcasters provided the balance" (Fore, 1977:21). Yet the same pattern persists today on both radio and television. This is important to remember when we assess the implications and significance of the electric church. Radio is, in fact, a growing factor in commercial religious broadcasting, and many broadcasters utilize both media as complementary techniques (Armstrong, 1981). Just as commercial radio sells television programs, religious broadcasters use radio to reinforce their television work.

The second consequence of this historical pattern is that the separate types of religious programming represent a deep and basic value schism within American religion (Fore, 1977; Armstrong, 1979; Marty, 1982). Those religious groups that are dependent on free time belong, on the whole, to mainstream, middle-of-the-road religions. It is misleading to refer to these groups as liberal, since there is considerable diversity within them. Commercial religious broadcasters are, on the other hand, independent, evangelical-fundamentalist organizations. Frequently, they are the very same organizations that were excluded from traditional arrangements for sustaining time. In fact, the NRB (National Religious Broadcasters) grew out of the National Evangelical Association's frustration with trying to surmount barriers to using radio and television (Armstrong, 1979). As the successor to the nineteenth-century evangelical-revivalism traditions, the NRB's initial purpose was to increase its members' access to radio and television. The difference in sustaining and paid broadcasts, therefore, represents two divergent and often hostile segments of American protestantism.

The Pacesetters in Television Revivalism

The early use of television by revivalists heightened and exacerbated these differences in origin and values. The early and successful adaptation to television by Billy Graham, Rex Humbard, Oral Roberts, and Robert Schuller was the beginning of the new hybrid electric church, and the value schism which this differentiation represents is extraordinarily clear and sharp. It was largely Billy Graham who, in the 1950s, facilitated the switch from radio to television. As a role model for other revivalists, he demonstrated the utility and applications of television as a "new measure" to stir religious enthusiasms (McLoughlin, 1959). Graham had been an established urban revivalist since 1947. On a trip to Portland, Oregon, in 1950, where he was conducting a revival "in a specially constructed tabernacle," he initiated "a weekly nationwide radio broadcast and a series of documentary and fictional motion pictures in which [his] revival sermons were the principal feature." These were radically new techniques. Up until then, "the only new technique which Graham had added to those of Billy Sunday was his use of a lapel microphone and a loudspeaker system in order to make his voice heard even when he whispered" (McLoughlin, 1959:492).

Graham's career has been a continuation of the lineage left by Sunday and other urban revivalists (McLoughlin, 1959; Gasper, 1963). His professional education and training were so embedded in this tradition that Graham even preached at Sunday's Winona Lake summer retreats as part of his early training in the ministry (Michael, 1981). When Graham used television, it was simply to augment his basic ministry but his doing so demonstrated the potential of the medium, and it made him a national celebrity (Gasper, 1963). In this respect, Graham was a role model for younger revivalists. At the same time, because Graham was also part of the evangelical-fundamentalist tradition, his career linked this tradition to the new media of radio and television (McLoughlin, 1959). With this one step, the religious tradition, which had lost much of its credibility by the 1920s, in the aftermath of the Scopes trial, gained new legitimacy and recognition.

Other evangelists such as Rex Humbard, Oral Roberts, and Robert Schuller also functioned as pacesetters in the electric church. Although Schuller is not a revivalist like Humbard and Roberts, all three men operate under the premise that the broadcasting medium is integral to their evangelical ministry. Early on, each wanted to expand his broadcasting. Television was never perceived as an addition to ongoing church activities. Instead, the use of television for all of these revivalists was intrinsic to the growth and type of evangelism which they practiced (Morris, 1973; Ellens, 1972; Armstrong, 1979). A brief account of the beginnings of each of these three ministries will illustrate this point.

Rex Humbard started his ministry in Akron, Ohio, in 1952, and from the beginning both radio and television were part of his ministry. The Cathedral of Tomorrow was built specifically for television broadcasting. It can seat five thousand people, and "its auditorium includes an impressive array of camera, sound, and lighting equipment" (Armstrong, 1979:82). There is sufficient room for crew, chorus, orchestra, and the fourteen family members (Armstrong, 1979:83–84). Humbard clearly built a media ministry.

Oral Roberts had established himself as "king of the faith healers" by 1952. According to Morris, Roberts drew large crowds and had a full organization to mail large amounts of literature. Roberts also "was on more radio stations than any other faith healer" (Morris, 1973). Rex Humbard urged Roberts to televise, which he did in 1954. By 1955, Roberts was the national leader of paid religious television (Morris, 1973:83), a position which he consciously worked to maintain (George, 1981) and lost only in 1983 to Jimmy Swaggart. With television, Roberts expanded his "Healing Waters" ministry into the Oral Roberts Evangelical Association, Inc. The story of this expansion is similar to accounts of the growth of small firms into modern, entrepreneurial corporations. From his original purchase of 175 acres of land in Tulsa, Oklahoma, for

$250,000 Roberts has developed a multimillion-dollar corporate operation. Part of this organization consists of the Oral Roberts University. Included in the university are a Law School, Medical School, Theology School, and Communications School. The City of Faith Hospital and Research Center is the most recent addition to this complex (Morris, 1973; George, 1981).

Roberts' fundraising techniques, developed early in his ministry, are a vivid example of the influence of television economics on programming. In order to raise $42,000 to improve the quality of his television production, Roberts instituted the "blessing pact." He asked 420 people to pledge $100, and he promised "if the Lord had not returned their gift from a totally unexpected source within a year, he would refund their money" (Morris, 1973;108–9). This fundraising technique Morris calls

Plate 4. Scene from a televised broadcast of a crusade service performed by Oral Roberts. Roberts made the transition to television during the 1950s. Courtesy Oral Roberts University.

"a success and prosperity doctrine" (1973;108–9) whereby the viewer is promised success or material rewards for contributing to Roberts' ministry. Tithing, which is a sacred obligation, was changed with this one innovation by Roberts. Now tithing or offerings were to be given with the expectation of material reward (Morris, 1973).

Robert Schuller, the third pacesetter, established his ministry in the 1950s in Garden Grove, California. He began a drive-in church and delivered his sermon from the top of a snack bar. The expansion of his ministry has been dramatic, and in 1981 he completed the building of the Crystal Cathedral at the cost of $16,000,000. Although Schuller is ordained in the Dutch Reformed Church, his dynamic and expansive evangelism appears to be self-directed and based on his entrepreneurial skills, in the same way Roberts' and Humbard's ministries were (Hurdle, 1981).

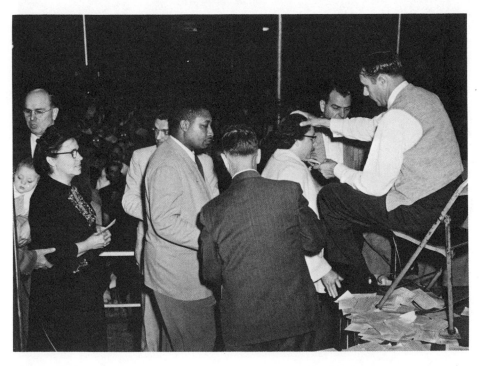

Plate 5. "Prayer for healing" during a service performed by Oral Roberts, 1952. Courtesy Oral Roberts University.

These three men, through their successful use of television, provided the impetus for the founding phase of the electric church. Their use of religious broadcasting began the reinstitutionalization of popular religion and was the basis for the developments that followed during the 1970s and 1980s. For the many broadcasters who followed them, they were significant others (Mead, 1974), role models for Bakker, Robertson, and less well known preachers who built their own evangelical organizations twenty years later.

The Ethos and Traditions of Urban Revivalism Adapted to Television

Finney's exhortation to revivalists to use "new measures to stir up emotional excitements" and to take an active role in winning souls is echoed by the attitudes and behaviors exhibited by Humbard, Roberts, and Schuller. All three men eagerly experimented with television as a "new measure." Once again, as in Finney's critical statements in *Lectures on Revivals of Religion,* an ethos of religious (revival) broadcasting initiated a new stage in the process of institutionalization. This time it was the addition of complex broadcast technology (the medium and the organization) that influenced and organized the process. These three pacesetters or "founding fathers" of the electric church immediately recognized the power of broadcasting to reach large audiences, the almost magical process through which a television program would generate thousands of letters and cash offerings, interpreted by the preachers as signs of the appeal's success, God's blessing and support of their calling.

With television as the major tool in their ministerial work, the evangelists' goals and decisions were placed within a new frame of reference. Subtle and incremental shifts and changes in their work followed. Television production required large amounts of financing. In addition to having to find ways to relieve some of these economic pressures, revivalists began to modify staff composition and organizational arrangements. Technical staff were recruited, often from commercial television, to write, direct, film, and produce programs. Details of syndication, distribution, and marketing had to be dealt with. The professionals who worked in these areas came from a different work culture than did other members of the revivalists' organization. Among them were the trained engineers, film makers, and cameramen, to name a few. This contrasts sharply with Sunday's staff requirements of a chorister and musicians trained within church-related organizations (McLoughlin, 1959).

This interaction between the revivalists and the broadcast professionals is a constant problem in the electric church. Many televangelists hire or contract with broadcast professionals whose technical training is in the secular sector (Lloyd, 1980; George, 1981); not surprisingly, their training and orientation support television practices over evangelism goals. To resolve this problem, Christian communicators are being trained for the electric church at Oral Roberts University, CBN University, the Heritage School of Evangelism and Communication, and the Moody Bible Institute, to name the most prominent schools.

Some organizational changes stem from the high costs of broadcasting. Expenses incurred in buying time, marketing, and production have forced the ministries into heavy fundraising activities. While some teleministries have financial backing, on-the-air fundraising is the primary means of mobilizing capital. From on-the-air fundraising, it was a short step for the teleministry to provide special services or tokens of appreciation for viewers. Tourist centers, bookstores, and recreational facilities were spawned, indirectly, to service viewers and over time, and more directly, to supplement the teleministry's income (Morris, 1973; Lloyd, 1980).

In addition to changes in staffing and organizational structure, the use of television profoundly altered the relationship between the revivalist and his audience. Before television, Oral Roberts went from town to town with his healing ministry, and his audience changed with every service. He could preach the same sermon over and over, and it would not be repetitious for his listeners. As the visiting revivalist, he knew that in each community people would eagerly come to hear him and see him. With the shift to weekly broadcasts, his preaching reached the same people week after week. He had to capture their interest over and over again and establish a permanent or continuous relationship with them. This meant that he had to maintain his personal integrity and credibility over time. This new relationship and the change in expectations between revivalist and audience forced the revivalist's role into a new context. In other words, the revivalists' style, persona, and appeals to the audience had to be modified for television broadcasting.

8

TELEVISION IMPERATIVES AND THE ELECTRIC CHURCH

> The television image is a constructed one, involving processes of extreme technological refinement and relying for its own effectiveness on complex systems of culturally determined message coding.
>
> (Beharrell, 1976:39)

To CONTINUE OUR ANALYSIS OF TELEVISION, the second parent of the electric church, we must understand the imperatives of television production, as well as the structural and value elements which directly influence televised messages. How messages are sent directly influences what is perceived by the viewer.

The expression *imperatives of television* emphasizes the point that television is not a neutral medium. As in any adaption of new technology, the introduction of tools carries with it new systems of work, changes in tasks, and ultimately changes in attitudes, values, and ways of organizing reality. For the electric church, the introduction of television implied a total reorganization of communication by the preacher and a totally new construct of religious reality.

Essential Characteristics of Contemporary Television

Contemporary television has three interrelated and essential characteristics that together account for the imperatives of television. These characteristics are: (1) the total message system and its components; (2) the requirement for producing the program; and (3) the packaging of the program or format. Each of these imperatives influences television's final product, that is, its program and its message. The electric church is no exception.

The message system and its components. Television broadcasts, or what the viewer sees and hears on the screen, are the end product of a complex socio-technical system (Emery and Trist, 1970). One way to envision the television message system (figure 1) is in terms of its four major subsystems or components (DeFleur and Ball-Rokeach, 1977; Cantor, 1980).

The production staff, as its primary task, organizes resources, shapes what is put on the screen, and determines what is left out (1). It is primarily through the work of this staff that a content or intended message is translated into a program (Elliott and Chaney, 1969; Elliott, 1973). The production staff's managerial tasks include planning, financing, distribution, and marketing of programs. Completion of these tasks links the production system to the messages or programs (Holsti, 1969).

The messages or television programs are processed by the produc-

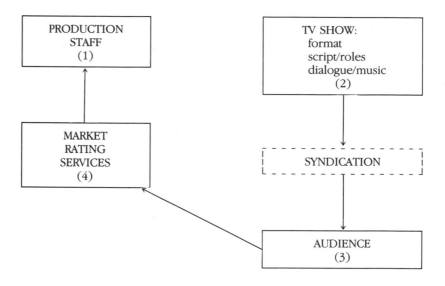

Figure 1. Schema of Television Message System.

tion staff with the intention of communicating specific meanings and ideas to viewers (Elliott, 1973; Gerbner and Gross, 1975). Nonetheless, as a general rule, one of the first objectives of the production system is to air programs which will attract large numbers of viewers. Television is an expensive medium of communication, and, in order to retain financial viability, the ability to consistently maintain large audiences for specific programming determines its economic health: commercial air time, whether purchased by General Motors or the Oral Roberts Evangelical Association, is expensive. This expense can only be justified by the sponsor or purchaser if television increases sales of its products or if television fundraising collects sufficient amounts of money to pay for costs (Lloyd, 1980). This cost/benefit justification is based on estimated or potential audience size (Owen et al., 1974; Barnouw, 1978). Just as Sunday demonstrated his effectiveness by counting the number of converts and calculating the cost at $2.00 a soul, the leaders of the electric church measure their success by audience size and market penetration (this measures the percentage of television markets which carry their programs and indirectly measures the potential number of viewers). These measures of success, of course, relate directly to the preachers' ability to maintain their television markets.

Programs attract audiences through the content and meanings embedded in the show itself. Here, production values—the use of technology, finances, casting, and other production decisions—influence the program (2). Expenditures for equipment, sets, writers, and musicians—decisions which contribute to a show's attractiveness to audiences—reflect these production values. What is said, who says it, music, sound, movement, and color are all part of the messages audiences receive.

How viewers react and what they are influenced to "buy" are also crucial questions for producers. The producer always keeps the sponsor and his product in mind (3).

Market research attempts to measure how effective each program is in reaching appropriate buyers for the sponsor's product (4). Generally, Nielsen and Arbitron rating services are employed to determine demographic information and the audience size, measured as viewers per household, or "VPH." The age range and predominant sex of the audience must be determined as well. This information is used by the production system and, in turn, influences program content. Demographic data about purchasers are known beforehand. The decisions, then, concern matching the program to the desired audience. Data from rating services help producers assess the "effect" of a program message on the audience (Goldsen, 1977; Cantor, 1980). Mail from viewers, comments from other television professionals, and independent market surveys all serve as feedback for the production organization. All television message systems, from "Dallas" to the electric church, operate in this manner. Moreover, commercial religious programming takes this formula even one step further by attempting to generate direct financial support from viewers (Armstrong, 1979; Lloyd, 1980). The producers of religious television have immediate, measurable feedback in the numbers of calls, letters, and amounts of money received. This is a distinct advantage over business sponsors, whose feedback is mediated by rating services, who measure only the numbers of television sets turned on and merely estimate the increase in consumer sales (Goldsen, 1977; Cantor, 1980).

However, this theoretical schema describes the television message system as closed or self-contained. It is not. Television is a subsystem: it is one part of our whole mass-communications system. Naturally, it is influenced by its position within that larger system (Parsons, 1951). The norms and values of the industry, the people who work in it, the regulatory environment of the FCC, and American cultural trends directly impinge on the message system and its operation (Gerbner and Gross, 1975; DeFleur and Ball-Rokeach, 1977; Cantor, 1980).

Figure 2 depicts the special message system of television ministries. It is basically the same model as that used in nonreligious television, the main variant being the electric church's use of direct mail for feedback and fundraising. The leaders of the electric church also use Arbitron and Nielsen rating services and incorporate this information into their programming decisions. Oral Roberts, James Robison, Robert Schuller, Jerry Falwell, Jim Bakker, and Rex Humbard have their own marketing departments and may also employ outside marketing professionals. CBN, which has been conducting its own research, reported at the NRB annual meeting in 1984 that these data influenced its use of "news" on the "700 Club." Because of this keen interest in who watches and how often, many broadcasters of the electric church contributed funding to the *Religion and Television* research project. From this, they hoped to receive richer and more detailed audience information than that supplied by Arbitron and Nielsen rating services.

Producing the television program. This second imperative of television consists of the activity on which the medium's personnel, organization, roles, and technology are focused. This is the development of the program itself. The task is to coordinate and use both human and technical resources to translate or interpret concepts into filmic images and coherent messages, that is, the program that is later broadcast by the local stations (Eisenstein, 1949; Millerson, 1961; Gessner, 1968; Madsen, 1973).

The television industry is market-driven and very competitive. One consequence of this is the rapid adaptation and use of new technology by producers of television programs, both in the nonreligious and the religious sectors. Professionals in the business want to be current and use state-of-the-art equipment, since this is important for their own status and congruent with internalized professional standards of performance (Pavalko, 1971).

The industry is constantly changing, as is the technology, but it is old enough to have conscious and explicit statements on how the production process operates. It has established technical guidelines to implement the process, that is, professional standards and procedures by which television programs are produced (for example, Millerson, 1961; Madsen, 1973; Wurtzel, 1979).

Television as a communication medium differs from the motion picture in that television producers and their staffs are the people in the

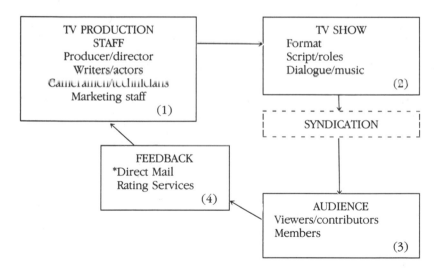

Figure 2. Schema of Television Ministry Message System.

organization who determine program content and final appearance. Films are creatively and artistically directed by an individual (although within criteria established by production decisions), while television programs are produced, that is, planned and packaged by a vast array of financial advisors, technological experts, and market researchers, all of whom contribute to a long chain of rationally calculated decisions (Goldsen, 1977; Cantor, 1980). The producer's role is to coordinate these segmented activities so that the finished product is coherent and effectively expresses the planned themes. The television production process controls the final output and, in fact, is similar to a small-batch manufacturing process with managerial control in the hands of the producer (Beharrell, 1976; Gitlin, 1979; Cantor, 1980).

The televangelists' programs are produced in the same way. As a rule, the production and marketing departments are separate from other organizational divisions of the teleministry. For example, the "Hour of Power" is a separate division within Robert Schuller's teleministry. Nason Media Corporation is responsible for the production and marketing of the program. According to a recent advertisement, Nason Media assists "the client" by providing "television directors and producers, public relations, marketing specialists," all to help "define the ministry" for the viewers (*Religious Broadcasting*, February 1985). As with any contractual arrangement, key people in the ministry have substantive roles in the production process. Mrs. Schuller continues to be part of the production team. Dr. Schuller continues to prepare his own sermons. The themes and messages for the "Hour of Power" are planned one year in advance, and Nason Media is an integral part of this process.

Every detail of the program—music, songs, guests, visuals, camera shots, and commercials—must be of a piece with Schuller's message. These are scripted by Nason Productions. While there is one producer, the program is manufactured by a sophisticated, socio-technical work team. The producer's role is to oversee or supervise the construction of the television image. This role, according to Cantor, is the most powerful one from both a managerial and creative standpoint (Wright, 1975:66).

A brief overview of the steps necessary in producing a television program explains how this image construction happens. The program idea or concept is generally developed in a five-step process. The five steps are "(1) analyzing the audience, (2) researching the program idea, (3) deciding on the production mode, (4) developing the treatment, and (5) preparing the program budget" (Wurtzel, 1979:479).

The key question which the producer asks during this process is whether the idea or concept is

> suitable for television and for my production situation...? In general, look for a program idea that will lend itself to television's visual capabilities.... On the other hand, what can you do to develop the show to take best advantage of television's unique qualities: its timeliness, its intimacy, its ability to closely involve an audience in a program? (Wurtzel, 1979:481).

A program "treatment" is a statement of the general format being proposed; it outlines the program. Within the television industry, the program treatment is a means of selling the program concept to financial backers. It precedes actual writing or filming. Included in the treatment is a description of the idea, its justification in terms of audience appeal, the production mode, and any other information necessary to specify the program idea (Wurtzel, 1979:484).

This "plan-to-sell" is a critical point in shaping the program since the resulting treatment will have been influenced by the expressed or implicit expectations of the television professionals, the commercial sponsors, and the television management (Elliott, 1969; Gitlin, 1979; Cantor, 1980). In addition to these specific influences, such general considerations as norms of good taste, attempts to avoid controversy, and reliance on easily recognized television routines and techniques also establish constraints which delimit specific program treatments (Altheide and Snow, 1979).

Once the program treatment has been determined, the producer's next task is to develop the format in detail. This detailed plan must convey the ideas of the program treatment through the types of characters, situations, and settings which were outlined by the proposal. It is at this juncture that technical details are contributed by writers, directors, camera people, and lighting technicians. A detailed scenario is drawn up to fit the format; roles and relationships are made specific; and finally, individual scripts are written for individual shows. By this time, the structure of the show has long been determined, and the writer is left "filling in the blanks" with action and dialogue. The cast is then selected, and rehearsals and filming can begin (Millerson, 1961).

Packaging of the program by using formats. The format is the conceptual skeleton upon which the program treatment is built, a frame upon which themes and ideas are built and transformed into filmic images. The use of television formats serves to classify the program for the viewer. Just as any container or box gives us a clue to its contents, the format or type of program establishes fixed parameters for the show which guide the director and create expectations for the viewer. Formats are basic units of the production process and permit standardization of content and routinization of production. "The Hour of Power" is a good example of a standardized church service. Its major elements consist of an opening hymn, musical offering, interview, and sermon. These parts are all interspersed with commercial-like fundraising appeals. The format prescribes the frame within which the show is constructed and helps determine the action, the type of characters, and the appropriate setting. What is omitted is, by implication, consigned to invisibility; what is seen becomes social reality (Gerbner and Gross, 1975; Gitlin, 1979). This standardization through "format and formula," according to Gitlin, is one technique by which "ideological hegemony is embedded" into programming. Gitlin explains this interrelation of form and content as follows:

> For commercial and production reasons which are in practice inseparable . . . the regular schedule prefers the repeatable formula: it is far easier for production companies to hire writers to write for standardized, static characters than for characters who develop. Assembly-line production works through regularity of time slot, of duration, and of character to convey images of social steadiness. (1979:254)

The format permits standardization of product and work process. It also limits the variety of products, which is an indicator of economic rationalization in the television industry (Weber, 1958; Gitlin, 1979). Standard program lengths are thirty or sixty minutes, and commercial breaks come at fifteen minute intervals. This facilitates standardization and packaging. Routine program formats and formula plots are symptoms of economic pressures on television production. They also manipulate and distort the social meanings of television for the viewer by focusing upon a limited number of social realities. Many segments of life are consigned to invisibility or unimportance, while others are given undue importance. This distortion occurs on all television programs, and viewers have come to expect drama or news tailored to fit preexisting categories. The natural flow of storytelling is disrupted and compressed to fit the standard time modules. In a process that operates in a manner similar to cognitive dissonance, if items do not fit, they are rejected as inappropriate or reshaped to fit the expectation (Beharrell, 1976).

Why has the industry practice of limited formats become embedded into the system? Certainly, the basic economic orientation of the industry, which was firmly established early in broadcasting history, accounts in large measure for this standardization. As an industry, television is an oligarchical, modern, corporate system (Owen et al., 1974; Monaco, 1978) with managerial pressures for budgetary supervision and control of the production processes to increase profitability. Decisions which, in the early days of television, were sometimes based on creative standards are now grounded in corporate budgetary considerations. In the same way, the televangelists, as they build national audiences, must have programs which appeal to wide mass audiences.

Concurrent with these considerations, managerial efforts to rationalize program production through the use of formats and formulas have facilitated management's control over personnel and fiscal policies. Today, television production work is fragmented and highly technical, so that no one individual is indispensable or irreplaceable. This has helped the televangelists build and run their complex organizations.

In addition to their utility for managerial purposes, standard formats also meet conditions for syndication or resale of programs. Syndication is an important tool for the industry as a whole, and it is especially important for television producers, who can earn additional revenue from syndication sales after the original network contract expires (Monaco, 1978). Syndication was critical in the growth of the electric church because it enabled the televangelists to build new markets. To the extent that the production expenses were fixed, the larger the audience, the greater the profitability or cost effectiveness.

Standardized programs that are complete within one showing are easily sold and used by stations that need to fill hours of broadcast time. One advantage is that these programs are interchangeable and can be scheduled as stations need them. A continuous series, such as a soap opera, is not as flexible since it must be broadcast in larger segments of sequential air time (Cantor, 1980). This flexibility also accommodates the needs of the electric church by enabling it to buy small blocks of time in a variety of test television markets before purchasing larger amounts of time and by allowing editing and scheduling of programs for specific television markets.

As critics of television programming frequently point out, this reliance on a limited number of formats and formulas tends to encourage bland, "least objectionable" content (Goldsen, 1977; Altheide and Snow, 1979) and, by inference, to discourage selection of imaginative or controversial programming. The networks, which determine the bulk of television programming, do not want to risk offending segments of their viewers. This, it is reasoned, would jeopardize audience ratings for that program, and since audience size sets the price of the air time sold to sponsors, networks will not buy programs which do not fit the mold or norm of "least objectionable programming" (Altheide and Snow, 1979). Some televangelists, such as Schuller, Swaggart, and Humbard, purposely avoid controversial issues so as not to limit their audiences.

Thus, the use of standard formats serves the industry's economic needs. These formats are embedded not in television as a technology but in television as a commercial enterprise. The imperatives are imposed on the technical system to meet the prior imperatives of profit making.

The Effects of Formats on Programs

The dominant format, according to Cantor (1980), is the episodic dramatic series. This form encompasses action shows, adventure programs, and situation comedies. All of these shows are constructed on a dramatic model: the action flows from a conflict, and the beginning, middle, climax, and resolution are scripted to fit neatly into the allotted thirty or sixty minutes, minus commercial time and station breaks (Millerson, 1961). "The series itself has a basic story concept that helps determine the content of each segment. This concept is usually relatively simple so that various complete stories can be told each week" (Cantor, 1980:28). Generally, there is a main character and several minor characters, whose relationships to each other are determined by the basic story concept and who reappear from episode to episode. "Magnum P.I.," "The Jeffersons," "Hill Street Blues," and "Alice" are episodic series based on Cantor's definition.

One consequence of the use of formats in commercial programming is "cloning" of shows, referred to as "spin-offs" in the industry (Goldsen, 1977:48–53). This happens when a basic formularized show is so popular that a secondary character is separated and given an entire show of his or her own. "After MASH" was cloned from "MASH," and "Rhoda" from "The Mary Tyler Moore Show." Jim Bakker's PTL Club was cloned from Pat Robertson's "700 Club." Bakker, however, uses a basic "talk-show" format, with music playing an important part. The "700 Club" is a mix of talk show and news-magazine format. This practice is also market-oriented. Producers attempt to replicate successful formulas by using familiar characters for a "new" show (Goldsen, 1977). This serves to reinforce the practice of standardization within the industry.

Formats, as already noted, ideally fit industry time norms, permitting station breaks and commercial insertions at set periods. Even Monday-night football games are played to fit the allotted time period with clocklike precision. Similarly, contemporary viewers unconsciously expect their news, variety, talk, and game shows to be cut and dramatized in predictable ways. The televangelists follow this same pattern by carefully scripting and editing their programs to fit their time and formats. This is accepted practice. Noting that "audience-interest or concentration patterns have to be contrived to be completely successful," Millerson diagrams the audience-concentration pattern for a program, break-

Plate 6. Ben Kinchlow (left) and Dr. M. G. "Pat" Robertson on the set of the "700 Club." The program format and context of this program is heavily influenced by secular television. Photo courtesy of the Christian Broadcasting Network.

ing down the action steps along a time line and carefully flagging the effect of the commercial interval.

> . . . we see where we hope to build tension, where interest will be allowed to fall. We see the attempt to grip audience-interest at the start of the programme, the minor variations, the build-up to an encouraging peak just before the interval (or commercial). The second half of the show begins with a bid to recapture interest, fluctuating with the story-outline, giving a build-up to the finale. (Millerson, 1961:334)

The structure of the show is no longer based on the intrinsic logic of the material but on the extrinsic, rationally calculated needs of the economic system that produces the show.

The most pervasive consequence of using standardized formats in commercial television has been the resulting reliance on a relatively small set of program formats. It is possible to categorize almost all adult programming into six formats: (1) episodic series, (2) news and current events, (3) sports, (4) talk shows, (5) variety or entertainment shows, and (6) game shows.

The eight leaders of the electric church use four of these categories in their program structures. The televangelists' programs are predictable, easily associated with the individual preacher, and standardized for ease of production. These formats help structure our perceptions of the preacher's role and enable the producer to select appropriate production elements—casting components, music, setting, color, and sequences—for translation into program messages. Once the pattern has been established, the viewer perceives a social reality, a frame of reference, which provides cues and symbols which the preacher uses to communicate his meanings to the viewer. These cues and symbols stimulate viewer perceptions and account for learning or socialization effects in symbolic interaction terms (Stryker, 1980). This is an interactive process. These associations enhance the viewers' sense of familiarity with the ministers, an association also encouraged by close-up television filming to make regular viewers of Oral Roberts or Robert Schuller, for example, feel that they are personally acquainted with these men. This same effect has been observed in commercial television (Altheide and Snow, 1979; Hadden and Swann, 1981). In addition to their social effects, these formats influence the program's story and messages. They convey meanings to the viewer. As elements of format change, elements of meaning also change (Beharrell, 1976; Goldsen, 1977).

Electric Church Formats in the Study

The programs of the electric church chosen for this study all have unique and distinctive formats, that will be described in some detail. All descriptions are based on shows aired between 1979 and 1982. All of the programs studied were units of small-batch productions. They were well produced and visually interesting and contained effective technical events. Programs deemphasized specific religious rituals, imagery, or symbols. Instead, they relied on visual imagery that was either naturalistic or ambiguous in connotation (Schuller, Humbard, and sometimes Bakker). Several shows used outdoor shots for background visuals, thus maximizing the potential of television technology for creating settings with generalized symbolic and secular appeal. These could be interpreted as "inspirational" and in the same tradition of popular religion as the examples analyzed by Schneider and Dornbusch (1958). Just as television programming observes the least objectionable norm when selecting content, the electric church shows are intended for a wide audience and not for a specific denomination audience.

The formats of the electric church demonstrate the influence of revivalism on their program content. It is clearly documented in this study, however, that these programs combine revivalist elements with television elements in distinctive proportions, so that their formats diverge from the ideal type of revivalism by varying degrees. Regardless of these differences, the dominant role of the preacher and the use of offering requests (or fundraising) are featured in all television shows of the electric church. The call for conversion is, significantly, the least used element. Table 1 shows how widely the elements of revivalism are used in the electric church.

Pat Robertson's "700 Club" has diverged most from urban revivalism. Of all the programs studied, it is the one most influenced by the imperatives of television. This show, which mixes talk-show and news-magazine formats, airs seven days a week in Philadelphia. During the period of this study, it was ninety minutes long. It appeared to be the most like secular television for many reasons. First, its preaching component is minimal. It is apparent that Robertson's role as a "preacher" has been changed for television: he has become a host. Although he may teach a segment, even using chalk and blackboard, the topics are often political or international matters. Robertson's presentations are low-key and informative, more like Walter Cronkite than Billy Sunday. His "direct" religious messages are usually embedded in commercial-like fundraising appeals and urge conversion and/or membership in the "700 Club." The program incorporates, in addition to talk-show interviews, filmed interviews and newslike coverage of human-interest stories. Topics or features may cover such "secular" interests as fitness, health, nutrition, investment advice, or family survival.

Although the seven other shows utilize the elements of revivalism to a slightly higher extent, they too show the influence of television on their formats. The programs are all scripted with television imperatives clearly in mind. They are episodic and continuous; one show is complete in itself, but elements carry over from show to show. As mentioned earlier, this is an important function of the building projects. They are visual and dramatic events for viewers to follow from week to week. Continuity is also achieved through the persona of the preacher and other regularly seen members of the show—children, wives,

Table 1
Uses of Revivalism Elements

REVIVALISM ELEMENTS	USES/MAJOR EMPHASIS	PARTIAL USE/ MINOR EMPHASIS
Music part of theme, prelude or bridge for preacher's message	Roberts Schuller Humbard Swaggart Falwell	Robison Robertson
Offering requests financial support	All	
Preacher dominant focus	All	
Message call to Christ/focus on religious change, conversion	Swaggart	Robison
Setting church, crusade	Schuller Swaggart Falwell	Robison

Table 2
Uses of Television Formats

FORMAT	STRONG USE	PARTIAL USE
Episodic/Dramatic Series	All	
Talk Show	Robertson	Robison Bakker Schuller
News/Magazine	Robertson	
Entertainment	Roberts Humbard Bakker	Swaggart Falwell Robison

announcer, and so forth. Family members are used regularly by all the preachers, with the exception of Robertson. Their shows are dramatic in construction, with the sermon serving as a point of emotional catharsis. The formats shown in table 2 reflect the influence of television usage on the formats of the electric church.

The analysis of these formats indicates a clear divergence, although in varying degrees, away from traditional revivalism formats toward more modern television formats. Furthermore, the messages of the programs do more than spread the gospel. This implies that imperatives of television are creating new goals and objectives, which, in turn, influence program content. Moreover, a greater number of formats exists in the electric church than there was in urban revivalism, most of them combinations of revivalism and television. This reflects thematic diversity among the eight preachers and is another indicator of not only new, but diverse goals.

Translating the Format for Film

After preproduction program-treatment and format decisions are made, the staff is faced with interpreting the concepts and moving into the actual filming of the program—a process of going from ideas to film images. In order to do this, they need the "language of film," that is, all those practices and operations which are part of making a film or television program (Millerson, 1961; Madsen, 1973; Mander, 1978). These professional production techniques are obligatory in the sense that they are perceived as essential to "good television." The unintended result of these practices is that filmic images are shaped or manipulated according to the objectives or intentions of the producer. In this step, meanings are organized and focused out of fragments of filmed action.

> Each scene is selected and edited into the film for what it says about the subject and that story at that point of the film. And a single dramatic action is photographed as many bits of action in different scene sizes, later to be edited into one movement, because its psychological impact may be heightened in editing by eliminating the superfluous and emphasizing first one detail and then another to make the edited action more vivid than the original action. (Madsen, 1973:42).

Although this is a critical technical aspect of television production,

> the physical act of splicing two pieces of film or videotape together is not editing. Film editing, as art and communication, is defined by the relationships between the content of two scenes, their internal movements, the screen directions of their subjects, their associated image shapes and the lengths of each scene used to create tempo. (Madsen, 1973:42)

It is the principle of editing or, to use Eisenstein's word, *montage,* that enables the editor to consciously and rationally yield the filmic effect. The following quotation from Eisenstein supports the proposition that this ability to edit is a rationally calculated filmic principle and that one should not "depend on 'intuitive creativeness' but on a rational construction of affective elements: each affect must be subjected previously to a thorough analysis and a calculation; this is the most important thing . . . a mathematical matter stringing elements together, creating dramatic tension (objective act)" (Eisenstein, 1970:14).

There are a variety of television-language techniques by which the producer imposes his vision on the screen. It is, however, assumed that the producer's perceptions reflect personal norms, values, and ideologic elements (Mannheim, 1936; Mead, 1974; Tudor, 1974). The techniques of television are the means by which influence, persuasion, or social control are used in attempting to shape the viewer's perception of the world. Cinematic techniques employ movement to suggest actions and relationships; editing presents logical sequences of activity and "meanings not inherent in the original content" (Madsen, 1973:28). Filmic techniques also "create a time and distance relationship only peripherally related to reality" (Madsen, 1973). For example, a story is seen as a logically and chronologically evolving series of events. This is a continuity not replicated in reality. The use of a sound track, dialogue, music, and other auditory effects to further the story line provides an emotional tone for specific effects. These techniques, along with lighting, framing of the picture, relationships among actors, background, camera angles, colors, points of view, and especially the dramatic structure of the show, focus and control the viewer's attention. They also make the program interesting and coherent for the viewer (Madsen, 1973; Mander, 1978). These television techniques have been adopted by

Plate 7. Videotape machines at the CBN Center, the Christian Broadcasting Network headquarters in Virginia Beach, Virginia. A technologically advanced broadcasting facility, the CBN Center produces the "700 Club" and operates a cable network as well as its commercial network. Photo courtesy of the Christian Broadcasting Network.

the televangelists. All of their shows are technically well done and comparable to commercial programs. Oral Roberts' programs are exceptionally attractive, but the most interesting to watch is the "700 Club" with its remotes and filmed inserts.

Thus, the technical implementation of the program format clearly impinges on the program message. The basic premise of the show rests on what can be filmed and, then, on how the filmed images can be shaped into a coherent series of scenes for the program. As explained earlier, the limited variety of formats reduces novelty in programming. This increases reliance on techniques called "technical events" to provide interest (Mander, 1978). Commercial television, according to Mander, is an "inherently boring environment, [and] producers create the fiction that something unusual is going on, thereby fixing attention. They do this in two ways: first, by outrageously fooling around with the imagery; second, by choosing content outside of ordinary life, thereby filling the test of unusualness" (1977:301). Mander argues that viewer attention is dependent on these television effects—the cuts, zooms, superimpositions, voiceovers, words on screen, action shifts, and sound changes. Commercial television programs use "eight or ten technical events for every sixty-second period. . . . There is rarely a period of twenty seconds without any sort of technical event" (1978:304). Advertising has almost doubled "technical action." Mander claims that "a thirty-second commercial will have from ten to fifteen technical events" designed specifically to make up for a sales pitch that is patently dull (Mander, 1978:305).

In addition to stimulating viewer interest in routine programming with technical events, television production relies on the personalities of individual performers to attract viewer attention. The innate immediacy of the medium draws the viewer into an intimate association with the performer. This transference or social interaction makes viewers perceive themselves as personally acquainted with the performers (Millerson, 1961; Goldsen, 1977). Such transference is not limited to the personality of the performer but extends to the program format as well; that is, individual actors become associated in the audience's mind with a particular format. Johnny Carson is a successful host and comedian, but he has been unable to transfer that success to motion pictures. In a sense, he is locked into his talk-show persona by audience expectations of his role.

Clearly, the technical imperatives of television are interwoven with the industry's economic needs. Only those concepts and ideas are transmitted which meet the criteria of "good television." As Mander points out, there is a programming bias toward "the more vivid, more powerful, more cathartic, more definite, 'clean' peaks of content. The result, not the process. The bizarre, rather than the usual" (1978:314). Mander argues that television demands "frequent catharsis, repeated high-light and achieved goals" (1978:316). "Content itself is usually chosen for its hyperactive effect. The survival of this dull, indistinct inherently boring technological failure called television depends upon this effect" (1977:317).

If this is the premise of television programming and content, how does this set of assumptions influence the programs of the electric church? The same imperatives that operate for television in general operate for religious programming; production decisions must be made to attract and retain audience interest.

Television production takes work, planning, and decision making. Ideas and messages must be translated into filmic images and sounds that make up a television program. This same production process applies to the programs of the electric church. (Indeed, one of the attributes of the electric church is the quality of its production values.) Despite justification and rationalization that the media are God's tools to be used for sending His messages, television has had a profound impact on both the messages and the means of producing them. The effect has been so profound that, after thirty years of religious television, we now have the hybrid organization, the electric church.

In creating this hybrid, the second parent, television, has transmitted a far more dominant set of genetic codes than did the first parent, urban revivalism. Television format, visualization, and commercialization are replicated in the hybrid offspring. However, the electric church's perceptions of itself as having effected a media switch denies the major influence of the television parent and instead emphasizes urban revivalism as the dominant parent.

Perceiving the electric church as a hybrid institution, on the other hand, provides us with a wide framework for explaining its growth. With this framework, we may ask, What are the major goals of this institution? How can we describe it? What are its roles and resources? And above all, what is its relationship with other institutions?

Before showing the impact of television production on the programs of the electric church and demonstrating that the electric church is indeed a hybrid institution, we should identify the institution's own frame of reference and contrast this to other perspectives. After this, other techniques to verify the existence of this hybrid, for example evidence of message changes, can be discussed.

Frames of Reference for Viewing the Electric Church

Branches of the electric church purport to be independent evangelical religious organizations dedicated to using the most effective and efficient tools of electronic mass communication to spread the "good news" (Armstrong, 1979). Simply stated, these broadcasters say that they are merely engaged in a media switch. They see their religious organizations as continuing established practices and traditions of American popular revivalism, using the electronic media to do so. The activities they engage in, they claim, are similar to those of the pretelevision revivalists, only modernized and updated for efficiency.

Today's broadcasters manifest their nostalgia and symbolic connection to nineteenth-century American religiosity in a variety of ways. The evangelicals frequently mention men who influenced their careers—Norman Vincent Peale, Billy Sunday, and Billy Graham—in order to establish a historical link between themselves and preachers of the past. This establishes a traditional legitimacy for their ministries. In addition to associating themselves with revivalists of the past, television preachers utilize their program formats to form nostalgic and sentimental associations. Ellens (1974) identified four variations of television formats, which he called "models." "Pulpits and prophets" features the preacher speaking "for and about God rather than enacting God's character and presence" (1974:66). James Robison and Jimmy Swaggart use this approach. Both rely on powerful preaching styles to engage their audiences. A second model, which is used by Oral Roberts, Rex Humbard, and Billy Graham, according to Ellens, can be called "Sinai and the spectacular." This is differentiated from "pulpits and prophets" by the smaller role that preaching plays. Preaching, in this approach, is purely one aspect of the "total spectacle" so that "the audience effect hangs not in the preaching, but on the total package" (1974:69). The third category, "electronic education," portrays Jesus as a teacher and is built on the tenet of Christianity that sees redemptive power in the ability to reach the truth. This differs from the premise of the first two models, which rest on "redemption in emotional crisis." "Electronic education" assumes that God is "friend, teacher, and Savior." This is the basic model used in Pat Robertson's "700 Club," in which talk-show participants teach and explain world events. The fourth model, "a little leaven," is a religious advertisement, similar to a commercial spot. During the 1960s, mainline churches used this technique widely, believing that it was cost-effective since it reached a large audience and was less expensive to produce than a weekly program (Ellens, 1974:126). This technique or model is used by Pat Robertson, Rex Humbard, and Jimmy Swaggart, within a program or in preprogram advertisements. The eight leaders of the electric church build their program formats on Ellens' religious broadcasting models, as identified in table 3.

The use of these descriptive categories, which are chronologically rooted in religious broadcasting techniques, provides meanings and associations for older viewers and links the televangelists with credible and legitimate popular religion practices. Both techniques—nostalgic connections and program formats—reinforce the church's claims of a media switch.

Table 3
Ellens' Models of Religious Broadcasting
as Used by the Electric Church

MODELS	STRONG USE		PARTIAL USE
Pulpits and Prophets	Robison		Swaggart
Sinai and the Spectacular	Roberts Schuller Humbard	Bakker Falwell	Swaggart
Electronic Education	Robertson	(700 Club)	Swaggart*
A Little Leaven			Robertson Humbard

*Note. Swaggart purchases weekday time and uses a teaching format. Programs coded were not of this type.

If, however, the electric church is not just a media switch but rather a new institution, a hybrid born of urban revivalism and television, it must be qualitatively differentiated from its parental antecedents. Are there, in fact, distinctive and unique characteristics which permit this differentiation? And if so, are those distinctive characteristics so profound that instead of seeing historical and evolutionary change, we can clearly identify significant social change?

The electric church is composed of independent, entrepreneurial, evangelical ministers working to "save souls." There is, however, another side to its work, namely the creation of many large, complex organizations adept at using modern mass technology and market-oriented techniques to stir "religious enthusiasms" and sell a political ideology. The traditional authority of the revivalist and his personal calling are no longer the basis for winning souls. Instead, modern, technologically sophisticated organizations have replaced the traditional authority of the revivalist. This represents a clear shift from charismatic authority to rational-legal authority (Weber, 1946). Rational-legal authority is based on rational decisions and those impersonal rules which are legally in place or part of the organizational situation.

How can this interpretation of the electric church's goals and authority be demonstrated? One way is to examine its program messages to determine whether any institutional changes are manifested in its broadcasts. The assumption is that virtually all television programs are the end product of the production organization and that program content indicates the intent of its producers (Beharrell, 1976; Elliott, 1979).

Using television as a tool of communication requires the command and diversion of large financial resources. Also, it is fair to speculate that the decision to employ these resources in this fashion has political or social objectives as well as evangelical goals (NRB Convention, Jan. 29, 1984). Thus, our working hypothesis is that the electric church has gone beyond a mere media switch, intentionally or unintentionally, consciously or unconsciously, and created a new institution with its own goals, objectives, and procedures for carrying them out.

In the next sections, we will adjust the focus of our sociological lens to analyze the impact of television on the leaders of the electric church. As part of the religious broadcast market, these preachers want to position themselves for their individual market share. To do this, they must differentiate their programs. They are not homogeneous, at least in terms of programs, as other researchers have assumed. Rather, they are differentiated among themselves by the use of a variety of persuasive appeals—all of which are different from urban revivalism.

PART IV

THE ELECTRIC CHURCH

9

THE VARIETY OF MESSAGES IN THE ELECTRIC CHURCH

> Access to television has given fundamentalism a power it never had before. It has once again become a social movement, and its vitality is now being restored.
>
> (Hadden and Swann, 1981:85–87)

THE PURPOSE OF OBSERVING AND CODING THE PROGRAMS OF THE ELECTRIC CHURCH is to determine whether their content differs from the content of urban revivalism. This information can then be used to determine whether we really have a media switch or a new institution. If the programs are intrinsically different and represent new or different goals and objectives, we have a new institution. If the programs are only extrinsically different, simply dressed up and updated versions of urban revivalism, we have an adaptation for television. The answer to this question is supplied in large measure by contrasting and comparing the television programs to urban revival meetings.

The forty-eight programs observed in the course of this study were broadcast in the Philadelphia area between May 3 and July 19, 1981. These shows clearly constitute definable units of communication and

Adapted from "Charisma and Old Time Religion in the Electric Church." Paper presented at the annual meeting of the Society for the Scientific Study of Religion, Knoxville, Tennessee, November 4–5, 1983.

105

provide observational boundaries for the sociologist. But even more importantly, they contain the major message sent by the preacher and received by the viewer. Through these programs, the preacher communicates with the individual. The entire show is, in fact, designed with elements to engage the viewer. Both urban revivalists and television preachers engage in parallel activities to save souls, but the latter have selected their elements to fit the imperatives of television. Our content analysis permits a specific historical comparative analysis. Although we do not have equivalent empirical evidence from urban revivalism, the ideal type of urban revivalism already described provides us with a way to relate it to today's electric church.

The Programs and Messages of the
Leaders of the Electric church

Let us compare three components of ideal-type urban revivalism—ethos, roles, and technology—with those of today's electric church. First, the basic ethos of television preachers is, in general, similar to that of the urban revivalists. Both are manifestly committed to stimulating religious enthusiasm by any means. The fact that today's preachers have spent their time and careers carefully honing modern broadcast technology demonstrates this commitment. In addition, these preachers have produced quality television programming through pragmatic experimentation and careful attention to preproduction and production decisions (Lloyd, 1980).

Second, it is apparent that the role of the television preacher is similar to the role of the urban revivalist. All these televangelists are energetic self-starters, high achievers, dynamic speakers, and skilled managers. They all claim strong religious callings that govern their career development. Urban revivalists and televangelists both place great emphasis on evangelicalism.

Third, unlike earlier urban revivalists, who were unitarily focused upon saving souls in an effective and businesslike manner, the leaders of the electric church express a greater variety and range of goals, a more sophisticated technology, through their activities and in their program messages. Oral Roberts has built a university. Pat Robertson established the Christian Broadcast Network and has built a university as well. If the electric church were a media switch, as these leaders argue, their goals should be a continuation of revivalist goals. We could expect slight variations, but essentially they should all be close enough to the mold to represent the same social phenomenon.

Hadden and Swann (1981) came to much the same conclusion in their study of televangelists and their variety of themes and social origins. Although Hadden and Swann did not conduct a formal content analysis, they found that, as a whole, televangelists are part of the same social movement as the religious Right. Moreover, much of their power comes from their ability to use television to mobilize resources. Stacey and Shupe, on the other hand, argue that there is differentiation among televangelists. Gerbner and his co-authors, in *Religion and Television*, divided the content of religious television message analysis into three large categories: (1) independent ministries (prominent and other), (2) mainline churches, and (3) miscellaneous. Their report, however, compared religious television with general television; thus aggregating the content of all religious television, they blurred distinctions within the first group of programs. The data in the present study indicate that there is no single type of preacher or program. Rather, there is significant diversity among the eight leaders, and this diversity can be ex-

Plate 8. CBN Center, Virginia Beach, Virginia. Photo courtesy of the Christian Broadcasting Network.

plained as degrees of diversion from old-time revivalism. The eight leaders of the electric church in 1981 were Oral Roberts, Robert Schuller, Rex Humbard, Jimmy Swaggart, Jerry Falwell, James Robison, Jim Bakker, and Pat Robertson. From a video file of these leaders' religious programs, forty-eight shows were selected (six from each preacher) for observation and content analysis to document their messages systematically. (See appendixes A and B for complete descriptions of the research strategy; appendix C for data analysis results).

Results and Discussion of Content Analysis

The televangelists exhibited three clusters of behaviors. These were characterized as (1) television imperatives, (2) charismatic leadership, and (3) cultural fundamentalism. A detailed report of the items in each factor is found in table 10 (in Appendix C). In this section, we will analyze the importance of these findings and discuss how they confirm the existence of the hybrid institution.

Television Imperatives. All of the behaviors that fell into this category are fundraising behaviors that stem from television rules, techniques, perspectives, and relationships. This is what Altheide and Snow (1979:35) called "television logic." The behaviors were the requests made to viewers (a measure of the number of financial appeals, an index of financial need); the announcer making the request (a television role); use of commercial spot format (a count of the use of television format); appeal to continue watching (needed for audience continuity, this reflects major relationship change between preacher and audience); and finally, the number of reasons used to appeal to the viewer (this reflects television's need for technical events).

Clearly, these fundraising practices are rooted in television imperatives. First, there is the pressing need to raise funds to purchase air time and to cover production costs. Second, religious fundraising, like other television programming, must develop and maintain its audience size. This is measured by the number of appeals, announcer requests, and use of the commercial format. Third, to keep the viewer interested, there is a large set of reasons for the viewer to contact the ministry (these range from supporting the teleministry to phoning in a request to go on a ministry-sponsored trip).

Bear in mind that religious fundraising practices on the air are not regulated by the Federal Communications Commission (FCC) or the Code of the National Religious Broadcasters. The Evangelical Council for Financial Accountability sets standards for ethical fundraising practices and monitors its members. Yet none of the television ministries in this sample were members. Furthermore, rules and restrictions for other television broadcasts that limit both commercial time and message content to protect the viewer from deceptive advertising do not apply to the electric church. Because the electric church is religious broadcasting, it is free to exercise its own practices. This, of course, has been a factor of contention among critics, who contend that the electric church is diverting resources from local institutionalized churches.

If the behaviors in the category of television imperatives are due to financial pressures, producers with a higher financial need would use more techniques to raise money during the programs. Of course, all the preachers require large sums of money to continue broadcasting, and it can be assumed that they are subject to funding pressures throughout the year to meet expenses for production and operating costs (Hadden and Swann, 1981; Lloyd, 1980). There are also special projects or unpredictable financial pressures which exacerbate the routine maintenance fundraising goals.

The strongest use of television imperatives occurred in Pat Robert-

Plate 9. Satellite dishes at the CBN Center. Photo courtesy of the Christian Broadcasting Network.

son's "700 Club." Robertson, during the period under study, expanded his programming and purchased state-of-the-art telecommunications equipment and facilities (Ostrander, 1981). In fact, during this period, the Christian Broadcast Network became a major network and production studio, which is certainly a signal of strong financial pressure.

James Robison's heavy use of television imperatives, according to members of his production staff, was due to Robison's plans to expand his predominantly Texan broadcast audience into a national audience. These plans included purchasing additional broadcast time and producing prime-time programs (Hurdle, 1981).

Naturally, the industry likes to sell time to those demonstrating the ability to pay for it. Viewed from the industry's perspective, air time generally must be paid for in advance. While established television preachers like Billy Graham or Oral Roberts might be able to negotiate or make their own financial arrangements with independent stations, a relative unknown such as Robison would have to prepay, preferrably for a specific number of weeks, since station program managers prefer to establish a schedule and run it with some continuity. The larger the religious audience, the more likely the station can sell the surrounding commercial time.

During this time, two other ministries relied on television imperatives, both because of immediate financial pressures. Oral Roberts was fundraising for the City of Faith, a multimillion-dollar hospital and research center. The viewer was asked to contribute to construction costs, as well as to help equip hospital rooms. Rex Humbard, who had been number two in the Nielsen rankings, was losing his market share to Jimmy Swaggart and Robert Schuller. Under serious financial pressure, he had recently cut his program to thirty minutes in an attempt to retain his market share (George, 1981; Ostrander, 1981).

The remaining televangelists did not rely on television imperatives as heavily as did Robertson, Robison, Roberts, and Humbard. During this period, Jerry Falwell made the building of Liberty Baptist College the focal point of his drive, but he used an integrated approach, personally requesting funds in his sermon. Swaggart, Schuller, and Bakker did not utilize television imperatives during this period.

These observations on the use of television imperatives as part of the program message suggest that the televangelist is strongly engaged in resource mobilization activities for his ministry. While this has always been a major task for both revivalists and televangelists, the techniques used by Robertson, Robison, Roberts, and Humbard are directly the result of television. Furthermore, television itself accounts for inordinate financial pressures upon these ministers, quantitatively greater than any pressures placed on Moody or Sunday for a week of revival meetings. One must also consider that the televangelist has a different set of goals than did the urban revivalist. Supporting an entourage of revival workers is qualitatively different from building a hospital and university for Christian healing.

Charismatic Leadership. These are six behaviors which together make up appeals by the preacher for the viewer to contribute money. Although the need is the same as in television imperatives, the persuasive appeal is based on different techniques. In charismatic leadership, it is the preacher's credibility and worthiness, his extraordinary qualities, which serve to motivate the viewer to support his mission (Bendix, 1962:300). This is analogous to Weber's concept of charismatic leadership, in which the relationship between leader and follower is legitimated by the leader's personal rather than impersonal (that is, bureaucratic) domination or authority (Bendix, 1962:300). Although Weber's analysis was developed prior to mass broadcasting, his concept can be applied here with equal force.

Charismatic relationships can be established with a mass audience through the use of radio and television (Altheide and Snow, 1979; Goldsen, 1977; cf. Merton, 1946). Merton described this process in *Mass Persuasion*. In his research, Merton posited that a critical factor in mass persuasion or mass domination through broadcasting is "the nature of the affective relationship between the person advancing the arguments and the person responding to them. The same lines of argument will often meet with quite varied responses according to whether they are put forward by those toward whom one feels sympathetic or antagonistic" (Merton, 1946:109). The affective relationship between preacher and viewer is a critical factor; according to Merton (who probably derived his theories from Weber's concept of elective affinity), effective appeals address motivations and predispositions of the audience (1946:109). In the case of the television ministry, the appeals consist of the preacher making the appeal, integrating the appeal into preaching, and appealing to the viewer's altruistic motivations and predispositions.

Altruism, as expressed by the televangelists studied here, includes requests for aid for unfortunate others such as refugees from communist countries, Germans without church affiliations, drug addicts, war victims, and so forth. General altruistic appeals were classified according to the intended use of the money and according to whether the recipients were domestic or foreign. It is this specification of altruism that signals changes in organizational goals and objectives. Four types of altruism were classified: (1) evangelism (propagation of Christian faith among unsaved people); (2) charitable works (providing food or medical care for the needy); (3) support of the moral crusade; and (4) support of political activities. The moral crusade referred to specific attempts to influence values and beliefs among non-Christian groups—for example, changing school curricula, campaigning against pornography, or fighting alcoholism. Moral crusades were part of the fight against secular humanist influences in society (LaHaye, 1980). Specific political activities included sponsoring legislation to reinstate prayer in schools, supporting congressmen, or influencing political party platforms (Liebman and Wuthnow, 1983).

In this case, the general meaning of Christian altruism has been reinterpreted. Altruism as a Christian offering is directed towards the poor or needy, and not for "moral" and political objectives. Putting aside for the moment any attempt at evaluating this type of fundraising, let us consider the significance of these appeals as an organizational change. In the period from 1900 to 1930, many Protestant evangelical groups separated over religious and cultural issues. During the period of urban revivalism, Dwight Moody and Billy Sunday were able to enlist the help of local churchmen in drawing members of Protestant groups and churches to their revivals. During Sunday's era, however, what Marsden characterizes as "The Great Reversal" changed the orientation of some fundamentalists. Direct political action was scorned by many orthodox or fundamentalist Protestant groups and, according to Marsden (1980), "relegated to a very minor role." The televangelists who fundraise for moral and political goals, therefore, are reversing "The Great Reversal."

This evidence of the electric church's moral and political fundraising is an important finding because stations that sell large amounts of air time to broadcasters from the electric church tend to justify their actions on apolitical, purely religious grounds (Shoubin, 1982). This position is credible only on the assumption that people involved in fundamentalism and in the electric church are nonpolitical. But this assumption cannot be made, since fundamentalism encompasses a wide range of political positions, including the far Right or, to use Jorstad's term, "ultrafundamentalism." The connection between the electric church and New Right organizations had already occurred by the 1960s, according to Jorstad (1970). This historical link is important for several reasons. First, it gives content validity to the identification of sociopolitical messages in the programs of the electric church. Second, it lends support to Hadden and Swann's (1981) position that the New Christian Right and the electric church are part of the same social movement. According to my research, fundraising for altruistic purposes has been redefined to include the political and moral objectives of the New Christian Right. Third, this tie between the electric church and the New Right contradicts the claim that the electric church is simply part of the continuum of traditional popular religion (Armstrong, 1979). Popular religion tradition is based primarily on inspirational messages and techniques for improving oneself and one's life (Schneider and Dornbusch, 1958; Parker et al., 1955). This tradition uses symbols of civil religion and may, by inference, transform patriotism into a sacred duty. Schneider and Dornbusch state:

> In this literature . . . we can say with very minor qualifications that basic economic, political, and cultural forms are not invoked as having a bearing upon the fortunes of the "self," either in themselves or in combination with other agencies. In effect, the world of society has no influence upon the individual and is *not* to be reckoned as important in any sense in the question of his religious destiny. The literature is also nearly empty of references to the Social Gospel. (1958:23)

Does this contradiction (use of charismatic leadership appeals) hold for all eight preachers? The behaviors of these preachers partially confirm the expected relationships. Four programs—Jerry Falwell, Rex Humbard, Oral Roberts, and Pat Robertson—are rooted firmly in charismatic leadership behaviors. All of the preachers establish strong personal relationships with their viewers, but these four used the technique most during the period studied.

Jerry Falwell's program shows the most significant and strongest use of charismatic leadership during the period of this study. He does not separate his two roles—religious preacher and political activist—on the air. Falwell is outspoken about his objectives in both areas and combines his personal and affective relationship with his audience with a set of shared political and moral beliefs to "sell" his predisposed audiences the idea of supporting his work (Merton, 1946). He is clearly using his television programs for communicating both religious and sociopolitical messages. For tax purposes, however, his preaching activities and his "Moral Majority" activities are handled by two different organizations. All religious audience data to date support the assumption that regular viewers agree with the messages sent by the teleministers and that the messages reinforce their previously held positions. Thus, when Falwell preaches, his moral and political appeals address feelings of ethnocentrism; that is, they reinforce shared in-group beliefs about moral righteousness.

On the other hand, the programs of Bakker, Swaggart, and Schuller emphasize personal redemption and social change through individual religious conversions. The born-again experience is far more important than ethnocentric or political remedies. Thus, these teleministers do not use the charismatic leadership appeal. Rather, Bakker, Swaggart, and Schuller preach in the tradition of Dwight Moody, who converted individual sinners with a simple and positive gospel message. "The 'Three R's' adequately summarized his central doctrines: 'Ruin by sin. Redemption by Christ, and Regeneration by the Holy Ghost'" (Marsden, 1980:35). While redemptive, nonpolitical religious leaders preach hostility to the devil, church denominations, big government, and other corrupt institutions in secular society, their messages as a whole are consistent with urban revivalism.

Cultural Fundamentalism. Taken as a whole, topics in this category are part of the cultural heritage of fundamentalism and support the political positions held by the New Right. They focus on social and political discourse and favor a return of old-fashioned patriotism (that is, unqualified American patriotism or superpatriotism). These items echo aspects of what Bellah called "civil religion," or God's covenant with America, and Stacey and Shupe's study, which found civil religion to be significantly associated with "media religiosity only among conservative" viewers (1982:299).

Appeals to patriotism and civil religion are interwoven with several tenets of political conservatism. There is support for free enterprise, including specific ultraconservative policy positions—free market competition as well as the dismantling of government regulation of business activities. Both of these positions have been vigorously supported by President Reagan.

Statements that favored a return to old truths and verities included nostalgia for better days as well as support for traditional sexual and family values (Himmelstein, 1983). While these values were often expressed in general terms, one item, opposition to homosexuality, was a specific coercive moral issue (Gusfield, 1976). While drug abuse, abortions, alcoholism, and life in the fast lane were all mentioned by the preachers, homosexuality was the most frequently cited moral issue during this period. This may have been the result of a limited observation period. However, this overt opposition to homosexuality strengthens the link between the televangelists and the social values of the Christian Right. Opposition to homosexuality is one aspect of the efforts of the New Christian Right to maintain the traditional family. These positions are major themes of cultural fundamentalism as an ideology of a social movement. While they have a historical relationship to theological beliefs, they also support political beliefs. Depending upon the political climate, they can be conservative or liberal.

If this interpretation is correct, only those religious programs associated with the New Christian Right should emphasize cultural fundamentalism. This statistical relationship was confirmed. The programs of three preachers (Jerry Falwell, Pat Robertson, and James Robison) strongly correlated with cultural fundamentalism. Preachers not showing these behavior patterns were not active political participants (Oral Roberts, Jim Bakker, Robert Schuller, Jimmy Swaggart, and Rex Humbard). Their programs speak to individual religiosity, personal needs, and satisfactions in the tradition of inspirational popular religion (Schneider and Dornbusch, 1958).

These variations in types of persuasive appeals support the original contention that the messages of the electric church are significantly differentiated. Since the research design assumed that the objectives of the producer determine program content (Cantor, 1980; Elliott, 1972; Gerbner and Gross, 1975), these differences in program messages are evidence of variations in goals and objectives among the leaders of the electric church.

10

THE USES OF TELEVISION

TV can be a marvelous means of communication, depending on who controls it. Fortunately, a courageous few—Jerry Falwell, The Radio Bible Class, Pat Robertson, Rex Humbard, and others—use it to communicate their moral and Christian convictions.

(LaHaye, 1980:158)

The Preachers and Their Messages

THE LEADERS OF THE ELECTRIC CHURCH ARE generally assumed, both by proponents and by critics, to have uniform and homogeneous viewpoints. The elements that unite them are thought to be their evangelical fundamentalism and their social-movement ideology. But these leaders are not uniform at all, as demonstrated by the variety of persuasive appeals and the way in wich these appeals are used by the eight televangelists in this study. What is the significance of this finding? Can we make a connection between these messages of appeal and the television ministries producing them? What can we infer from these messages about their intended audiences?

An analysis of the shows produced by the eight teleministries generated a twofold typology (cf. Table 4): one type of show did not use persuasive appeals (Jimmy Swaggart, Jim Bakker, and Robert Schuller); a second type did use these appeals, but in slightly different combinations, (Oral Roberts, Rex Humbard, James Robison, Jerry Falwell, and Pat Robertson). If the variations in thematic patterns are interpreted as diversions from urban revivalism practices, or to put it another way, as

116

responses to the imperatives of television, then the programs fall on a continuum ranging from urban revivalism to television dependency. This relationship is diagrammed in table 4.

Those programs not using persuasive appeals have diverged the least from urban revivalism. These preachers speak directly to the traditional needs of individual religiosity. Viewers are given hope, comfort, and directions to ease the pain of a variety of personal problems. Inspirational messages and personal prayers are part of the televangelists' message, and the preachers often tell their viewers to lead a renewed and hopeful Christian life. One unifying theme among these televangelists is the individual's reliance on personal change and religiosity as a technique for improving his or her life. This is the same popularized version of religious behavior that has been promulgated to mass audiences since Finney's revivalism. The message of many American revivalists, as well as a rich body of popular religious literature (Schneider and Dornbusch, 1958), can be categorized as inspirational. Individuals have the choice and the ability to change their own lives. No one has been selected as a chosen one. Thus, what McLoughlin identified as the democratization of salvation is very much manifested in these programs. These personal appeals to individual choice were interpreted by Hadden and Swann (1981) as privatized religion, a kind of religiosity that fits the needs of the alienated, consumption-oriented television viewer.

In direct contrast to inspirational religion, at the opposite side of the continuum, Pat Robertson's "700 Club" used all three persuasive appeals (television imperatives, charismatic leadership, and cultural fundamentalism). As mentioned earlier, Robertson diverged furthest from traditional urban revivalism. His programs are also the most influenced by television. This has been confirmed by Robertson's own recently published statements (Clark, 1985; Traub, 1985), in which he views himself as a broadcaster, rather than a televangelist. Robertson has always separated himself from other religious broadcasters and has not wanted to be classified as a fundamentalist. Despite his statements, however, his programs strongly support and reinforce the moral positions and the political planks of the New Christian Right—from family issues to aggressive political action in Latin America. He is antifeminist, antihomosexual, antiabortion, and antiunion.

The remaining four televangelists (Oral Roberts, Rex Humbard, James Robison, and Jerry Falwell) use appeals in a different manner. Oral Roberts and Rex Humbard rely a great deal on television impera-

Table 4

Types of Persuasive Appeals Used by Leaders
of the Electric Church

CONTINUUM OF TELEVISION INFLUENCE

POPULAR RELIGION ←——————————————————————→ MASS PERSUASION

Inversely Related to Scales   Directly Related to Scales

Values and Themes in Religious Messages

Inspirational, popular, and pesonalized religion	Popular and personalized religion. Personal attack on social institutions—no remedies	Popular, personal sin stressed. Moral reform a remedy.	Moral reform and changes in social institutions as remedies.	Moral, reform, social, and political institutions need to be changed.

Preachers Using Each Type of Appeal

Jimmy Swaggart Jim Bakker Robert Schuller	Oral Roberts Rex Humbard	James Robison	Jerry Falwell	Pat Robertson

tives and charismatic leadership. Both are senior members of the electric church and among the first preachers to establish and build large facilities for their television ministries (Morris, 1973). These preachers project a paternalistic image. They put their families on their shows and speak as heads of these families while they are addressing the personal needs of viewers. This strategy reinforces their own credibility as respectable and authoritative men. It also symbolizes their support of "traditional" family values. Oral Roberts, who started as a healer, has updated his image to become the builder and chief executive officer of the university and medical complex that bear his name. His viewers are asked to send "seed faith" money, and, in return, he promises to heal physical, spiritual, family, and financial problems for the viewer.

Rex Humbard establishes basically the same relationship with his audience. He builds on his paternalistic image and asks his viewers to

Plate 10. Oral Roberts' son Richard and the ORU Singers; "Celebration with Oral Roberts," a primetime special marking the opening of the City of Faith Medical Center in Tulsa, Oklahoma, 1981. Featured on almost all programs, Richard Roberts is being groomed to take over the evangelical ministry. Courtesy TRACO, Inc.

join the "prayer key family." His television images show many viewers alone—widows without families, mothers writing to children—evoking a sense of fatherly concern for the viewer. The message is: "Join my prayer key family, and you will not be alone. I will pray for you in return for your financial gift to my ministry."

In addition to fundraising appeals, the programs of Roberts and Humbard were made up of traditional popular religion elements: inspirational music and inspirational messages with no particular ideological appeal. Social or moral issues were discussed as general societal decline rather than as political problems with specific solutions. Humbard railed against the "great waves of sex" sweeping the country, or he addressed the problems of old age and loneliness. He never mentioned social or governmental issues. He spoke to the individual as an individual.

Both Roberts and Humbard made full use of their personal charisma, in the Weberian sense. Their message implied: "Follow me because I have been successful in the past. I have healed many people: I have helped others who helped me." In addition, Roberts continually reiterated his close relationship to God and that he was told by God to build the City of Faith. Both men are well-established televangelists, legitimated by past performances and successes. Neither, however, rests upon his laurels. Both regularly update their programs with new backgrounds, settings, and television techniques.

The objective of Roberts and Humbard is to maintain their independent ministries and to build their institutions. James Robison, by contrast, relies on a combination of television imperatives and fundamentalism to preach stridently against the personal and social sins ennumerated by the New Christian Right. He opposes abortion, gay rights, denominational churches, big government, and the media and favors "coercive reform," to use Gusfield's term. Robison, as a member of the "Religious Roundtable," is articulating the political agenda put forward by that group for the New Christian Right (Hadden and Swann, 1981).

Jerry Falwell's message combines charismatic leadership with cultural fundamentalism in much the same way. Falwell attempts to build a personal following while exhorting his viewers to moral and social reform—clearly not in the tradition or example of Dwight Moody's salvation revivalism. Falwell, it should be mentioned, has reversed his own early position of complete political disengagement for the clergy. By the 1980s, Falwell's television exhortations for political and moral change were totally in keeping with his newly acquired role as leader of the "Moral Majority." Although these two organizational roles are legally separated, his television role, in practice, attempts to influence viewers toward coercive reforms. There is considerable empirical evidence to show support of religious television and reinforcement of political strategies.

This raises some serious questions concerning television practices. While there is no question that all American television programming reinforces the status quo, or the American way, most programming does not take a direct political position. In this sense, the "Old Time Gospel Hour" violates television practices. At the same time, norms of religious broadcasting are also violated. Broadcasters usually tolerated fundamentalists as long as they shunned political involvement. Now, their new political messages violate the sense of fair play on the air that religious broadcasters have always honored in the past. This is especially critical because the electric church dominates the religious television market and is continuing to expand.

Whether a television program falls into the inspirational popular-

Plate 11. Scene from the "Old-Time Gospel Hour," featuring Jerry Falwell. Falwell began broadcasting in the 1950s from a television studio. Courtesy Old-Time Gospel Hour.

religion type or the influenced-by-television type, it is generally manufactured in small batches to attract particular market mixes or audience
segments. Regardless of where a program is on the continuum, it has
undergone some degree of transformation of message as a result of
television. The three programs closest to urban revivalism (Swaggart,
Bakker, and Schuller) have undergone the least transformation, the
"700 Club" the most.

Plate 12. Jerry Falwell in the 1980s, broadcasting from Liberty Baptist Church.
Courtesy Old-Time Gospel Hour.

What accounts for these variations in program messages among the leaders of the electric church? There are two possible hypotheses that explain some of this variation. Each is derived from program observations and fieldwork. One hypothesis is that market competition is the most salient factor influencing program messages (Barnouw, 1978; Goldsen, 1977). This assumes that all production decisions stem from the need to retain market share or to increase the audience size in order to maintain organizational income. Product differentiation is a common marketing response to such demands. For example, when Oral Roberts hired Kroft Productions to produce his show, rather than using his own staff, his decision was based on the need to retain his position as the number-one religious television minister. The change turned out to be unsuccessful, and Jimmy Swaggart became the top-ranked televangelist.

A second hypothesis is that the organizational goal—that is, the producer's interpretation of the teleministry's goal—is the most influential factor in message production (Elliott, 1973; Gitlin, 1980). While this premise is similar to the first one in that all teleministries must be concerned with maintaining market share, this mindset implies that producers incorporate ideological objectives as well as economic ones into their programs. The difference between these two hypotheses is exemplified by the following questions: Do you produce the show to be seen in 98 percent of the television markets because that will assure you of cash donations and a quality mailing list; or do you want your show seen in order to build name recognition for the televangelist?

Regardless of which set of factors is the most influential, it is the intended audience of each program that, in large measure, determines program content. Program producers orchestrate content and thematic differences to appeal to their audience characteristics. There is ample evidence from interviews with members of marketing and production staffs to suggest that the programs of the electric church are purposely constructed to solicit carefully defined audiences for financial and personal support. Songs on "The Hour of Power," for example, are selected for their inspirational message and then edited for an upbeat tone and the appropriate length. The producers know their audience—both from market research and from monitoring the kind of mail they receive.

One problem for these teleministries is that if they wanted to appeal to another market segment, they would require structural format modifications, particularly in the role played by the preacher. These changes might lose them their existing viewers. Oral Roberts faced this dilemma when he followed Kroft Productions' suggestions. One innovation, for example, involved using puppets to reach younger viewers. While the approach may have been successful with the young, Roberts ran the risk of alienating his older supporters.

The business of retaining audience share is a structural change in the preacher's role. It indicates that the infrastructure of the institution has been changed. Indeed, this again is evidence that the electric church is a new, hybrid institution. The revivalist's new role is to manage, produce, and direct his television program.

The Preachers and Their Audiences

Thematic differences in the electric church reflect the marketing strategy of product differentiation. This strategy assumes that all products, in this case televangelists instead of laundry detergent, are basically the same and that program packaging is the producer's main means of competing for a share of the market (McCarthy, 1978). At the same time, demographic differences in viewers are critical since pro-

Plate 13. Scene from "Celebration with Oral Roberts," 1981; shown are Oral Roberts and Kroft puppet. Courtesy TRACO, Inc.

gram changes are made to attract specific audience segments (men, women; age 25–54, 55 +, are examples of demographic segments).

If the teleministries are using a product differentiation strategy, then the themes should be distinctive enough for each preacher to enable the viewer to differentiate their themes. The results of this study lend credence to the product differentiation interpretation; however, the need for additional research in this area is clearly indicated. For now, we will focus on the relationship between the audiences and the persuasive appeals used in the programs of the electric church.

The largest market segment for the electric church consists of women over fifty years of age (Buddenbaum, 1981; Hadden and Swann, 1981; Stacey and Shupe, 1982; Gerbner, et al., 1984; Clark and Virts, 1985). Gerbner and his colleagues describe viewers of religious programs as "women, non-whites, old people, the less well educated, and those who make less money" (1984:89). These findings are consistent with the Nielsen data and with interviews conducted for this study (at Oral Roberts Evangelical Association, Robert Schuller's "Hour of Power," and James Robison's Evangelical Association).

This finding is, of course, congruent with the more generalized observation that women tend to be more religious than men. In particular, according to Buddenbaum (1981), women are more influenced by the personalized help offered by religious broadcasts. This insight has been confirmed by audience data from the *Religion and Television* research, which also reported that viewers watched religious television for the same reasons that they went to church. The reasons they gave were "the sermons, the music, inspiration and feeling close to God" (Gerbner et al., 1984:77). Therefore, an expected finding in our data would be that the three popular inspirational programs would have the largest female audiences, while the programs with political or fundamentalist messages would attract a smaller proportion of women viewers. It would also be expected that those programs with overt political messages would appeal in greater proportion to men and to a younger age group of viewers (both men and women).

These relationships were found in the audience data. Those programs relying on fundamentalist appeals are not as appealing to women in general or to older women in particular. Women support the popular religion programs over the newer types of programs. Although these findings are not statistically significant, they do tend to support the expected relationship.

These correlations may clarify in part what at first appears to be a

paradoxical situation. Indeed, if older women view and financially contribute to the electric church, we cannot assume that this association is
uniform among all the leaders of the electric church. In fact, variety in
the program messages is associated with diversity among the viewers,
or alternately the producers' perceptions of diversity among viewers
may account for this variety in the messages. The actual time of broadcast influences audience demographics. Since the "700 Club" is a daily
program, and Jerry Falwell's "Old-Time Gospel Hour" is a weekly program, there will be audience variations as a result of scheduling. In all
likelihood, Roberts and Humbard, who do not express fundamentalism
in their programs, attract a larger share of women viewers than do
Swaggart, Bakker, or Schuller. James Robison, Jerry Falwell, and Pat
Robertson all express fundamentalism, and as a result, their programs
are not as likely to appeal to women viewers.

The implications of these general findings are interesting to contem-
plate. If we assume that the religious broadcast market is finite, and the
largest segment continues to be composed of traditional women over
fifty years of age, a number of consequences can be anticipated. The
popular religionists will retain their share of this market, but since they
are operating under conditions of intense competition from other television broadcasters, we would expect increasing pressures for better
production values. In addition, if market concentration continues, a
smaller number of teleministries will have the largest proportion of
television viewers.

Those religionists expressing strident fundamentalism are put in
jeopardy of losing part of their market, the traditional women. This
means that they must compensate in some manner to retain a sufficiently large share of the market and be self-supporting (George, 1981;
Lloyd, 1980). If we assume, however, that the religious broadcast market
can be broadened to include demographic segments not served now,
such as men and a younger segment of men and women, then the
nontraditional appeals may attract these broader market segments as
viewers. The Gerbner data hint that this has already happened. The
Clark and Virts data further support these generalizations. While older
women still compose the largest segment of viewers, there is more
diversity than was apparent from the older Arbitron and Nielsen data.

There is an irony in this strategy. These new groups of male and
younger viewers will be receptive to religious programs that are "more
like secular television." If this is so, it must be asked at what point these
programs become secular and cease to be religious television. This, in

fact, is an issue for the Christian Broadcast Network, which now even goes so far as to attempt to market a "Christian" soap opera (Ostrander, 1981). And, in January 1986 CBN began producing its own news show.

Some religious programs have already passed the point of secularization on the continuum of television influence. The message-system analysis demonstrates that programs are a blend or composite of religious traditions, civil religion, and overt political viewpoints. An important point drawn from this analysis is that general assumptions about the religious phenomenon of the electric church, its role, and its intended audiences must be specified, since some of the televangelists have placed explicitly political messages under the banner of old-time evangelical religion. Are these preachers using their television programs to recruit potential followers? Are they using their technological and financial resources for their own political purposes? Are they preaching the gospel on public-service air time to advance New Right politics? In view of the two basic types of persuasive appeals, are those televangelists who continue in the popular religion tradition of urban revivalism more concerned than others with individual sinners? Are they too marketing the gospel in a manner influenced primarily by market imperatives?

This overview of the diversity of messages corroborates in a systematic fashion a number of interpretive impressions regarding the programs of the electric church. First, there are at least two types of messages coming from the electric church: popular religion and cultural fundamentalism. Second, compared with urban revivalism, all these programs deemphasize salvation and redemption. This is an expected corollary of the first point. And, finally, for five of the eight leaders, the use of television implies more than a simple media switch from urban revivalism. These leaders are operating within new institutions—a fact that is most poignantly demonstrated by the televangelists' approaches to fundraising.

11

FUNDRAISING
TELEVISION'S TRANSFORMATION
OF A RITUAL

THE EIGHT MINISTRIES IN THIS STUDY have been televised nationally for between five and thirty years. Through most of this time, they have managed to retain their relatively high market positions, partially because they know what is effective in generating funds. Lloyd (1980) studied Oral Roberts, Rex Humbard, and Jerry Falwell's production organizations and documented the rational calculations that are made to produce funds.

Fundraising is a major task of the technology of saving souls and television market shares. It is the television equivalent of the free-will offering of the urban revivalist. Fundraising is a specific task, part of a religious rite in its own right for all traditional and modern religions. In 1978, electric church programs made up approximately 92 percent of the religious broadcast market and generated over one billion dollars in contributions to support broadcasting activities (Armstrong, 1979; Cole and Oettinger, 1978a; Mathews, 1980). The public has limited access to the financial records of these organizations, and it was well beyond the scope of this study to trace this information. We do have, however, sufficient evidence to make intelligent inferences about the

Adapted from "Television and Popular Religion: Changes in Church Offering." In *New Christian Politics*, edited by D. Bromley and A. Shupe. Macon, GA: Mercer University Press, 1984. Reprinted by permission.

range of these activities, the monies spent, and the process of fundraising in these organizations.

It is noteworthy to add that we are in a period in the development of many of these institutions where several televangelists may no longer be television-dependent for their operating costs. Past fundraising efforts have enabled them to build and develop alternative sources of income. For example, Jim Bakker has been developing a multimillion-dollar complex called Heritage Village, U.S.A. At this time, the complex includes a school of communications, camping facilities, a television production studio (geared to commercial and other clients), and a luxury hotel. If these ventures succeed, they will generate additional income for Bakker and may well enable him to become self-supporting. Television fundraising will be only one income source among several.

This type of diversification and commercial expansion also applies to Schuller, Swaggart, Robertson, Roberts, and Falwell. Of course, these financial enterprises then become subject to risks and environmental influences just like other businesses. Changes in economic conditions, poor management, overexpansion, and competition are all factors that can jeopardize these enterprises.

Regardless of the outcome of these developments, the fact is that these preachers have, with the exception of Robison, demonstrated tangible signs of success. They have established large organizations, have engaged in multimillion-dollar building projects, and have had access to (owned or rented) state-of-the-art television production facilities and staff.

Another sign of success among the preachers is their personal life styles. None of these ministers lives an austere and ascetic life. They appear, at least in the image conveyed by press and television reports, as affluent corporate chiefs—wearing custom-made suits, traveling in personal jet planes, and living in comfortable and well-furnished homes. Several preachers claim that these amenities are gifts from friends of the ministry, and this may be true, but the impression is still one of extreme affluence (Sholes, 1979). Of course, in evangelical circles affluence can be interpreted as a sign of success, for it reflects the large number of souls the "wise minister" has saved.

Fundraising by the Electric Church

Fundraising by the electric church is a pivotal activity directly related to the televangelists' ability to improve their television markets and their organizational growth. However, as noted before, successful fundraising increases the likelihood of controversy and conflict with other religious institutions. The expansion of the electric church through the purchase of additional broadcast time is viewed as further displacement of noncommercial religious programming. It is clear that both groups perceive the situation in religious programming as a zero-sum conflict.Those in the noncommercial sector genuinely fear that if they lose access to television broadcasting, commercial broadcasters will gain an ideological hegemony (Avery, 1977; Fore, 1980a; Hadden and Swann, 1982; Marty, 1982; Mathews, 1980; McBrien, 1980). For noncommercial broadcasters who depend on sustaining air time, more commercial religion on television means less air time available to them. And if this is a correct interpretation, policy changes on their part may be necessary. Either they will have to purchase air time in a competitive market, or, as an alternative strategy, they will have to exert political pressure on local stations and on network affiliates to curb the amount of commercial religious programming. However, these possibilities are unlikely in the immediate future, as there is disagreement among television executives at all levels on the appropriate response to the electric church (Fore, 1980a; Hadden, 1980a; Parker, 1980b).

Not only is there no serious political challenge to the expansion of the electric church, there are also several environmental factors, some already noted, which have enhanced the electric church's ability to expand its mass broadcasting. One of these factors was the recent modification of network policy to permit commercial religious broadcasters to buy air time from local network affiliates. Another was a 1960 change in FCC policy to permit local stations to log commercial religious broadcasts as community sevice programs for licensing renewal (Lacey, 1978; Mathews, 1980). Lacey (1978) maintains that as a result, commercial religious producers have been federally subsidized. Under FCC policy and under federal tax law, these broadcasters are classified as religious, nonprofit organizations. Their nonprofit status benefits them in terms of operating costs and because it makes contributions to them tax-deductible. In addition, being nonprofit, they are not limited in the amount of air time they can use for fundraising or by standards set for commercial broadcasters by the National Association of Broadcasters.

The third environment factor in the expansion of the electric church was caused by the local stations' efforts to compensate for the revenue they lost from tobacco sponsors (Ostrander, 1981). This too was discussed earlier. Finally, the fourth factor in the electric church's growth is that, generally speaking, the production quality of evangelical programs is more professional than that of locally produced programs. For this reason, many independent stations prefer to air the commercial evangelicals (Bleum, 1969; Parker, 1980a; Shoubin, 1982). Denominational producers are not able to compete with the professionally managed programs of Jim Bakker or Pat Robertson because they do not have funds available for this purpose.

One issue revolving around fundraising by the electric church is stewardship of these funds. This is a basic question of values: How do you use the gifts and offerings received to enchance the Christain mission? Stewardship has sacred implications in church practice because it is connected to the obligation to tithe, that is, to give 10 percent of one's income to the church. The free-will offering, or passing of the plate for contributions, is incorporated into the liturgical service as a ritual act. It is part of one's sacrifice to God. Funds collected this way are used for a variety of church-related purposes—support of the ministerial staff, operating expenses, and charitable works. How church funds for "faith and works" are allocated varies, of course, from church to church and group to group. The allocation of funds for faith (the church and administrative overhead) and works (outreach and charity) has aroused controversy throughout church history (Moberg, 1962). Billy Sunday had his financial critics just as the televangelists have theirs.

Television ministries spend money on a wide range of activities, including air time, production costs, marketing religious mementos, tourist centers, educational facilities, and political lobbying. Such expenditures disturb noncommercial religionists' notion of Christian stewardship. They argue that too much money is spent on broadcasting in proportion to the amounts used for the delivery of "works" to the needy. This allocation of resources violates many American's belief in ascetic Protestantism. These people want less money spent on administrative expenses and more spent on the delivery of church services.

The serious controversy surrounding these fundraising practices remains. The Gerbner report which was completed after the research reported here did not provide useful empirical data. In the present investigation, programs were observed to determine the amount of air time devoted to financial appeals, the format of these appeals, and the motivational basis of the appeals. The findings from these observations were then used to compare urban revivalism to the electric church.

Televangelists and Fundraising

Fundraising categories, or "request to viewers to contact the ministry" included four major classifications: (1) air time spent on requests; (2) casting, or who made the request: (3) format, or how the request was structured; and (4) the motivational basis of the appeal (Holsti, 1969; Krippendorff, 1980). Figure 3 in Appendix B ("Requests to Viewers") shows the data sheet used.

Unlike earlier revivalists, the television preachers cannot directly solicit and receive money by passing the plate. The television screen intervenes. The preacher must adapt to this circumstance by asking viewers to contact the ministry either by telephone or by mail. Enticements, pleadings, and urgings must motivate viewers to take one of these actions if fundraising is to be effective. Once the contact is made the ministry obtains a name and address, an important resource for direct-mail solicitation. Direct mail is a major fundraising source for many televangelists (Ross, 1982). In addition, viewers often send a contribution along in response to the appeal. This behavior rests on the norm of reciprocity (Gouldner, 1960), whereby viewers feel obligated to contribute after they receive something from the ministry.

All the programs are carefully scripted, and their fundraising segments are constructed to conform to the image that a particular ministry has created for itself. Observations of programs document consistent relationships between the themes of the ministry and the nature of its fundraising appeals. Most of the ministries use market-research techniques to evaluate the effectiveness of their programs (George, 1981; Hurdle, 1981; Lloyd, 1980). Each ministry establishes its own financial rule-of-thumb to determine whether or not its program is self-supporting in a particular television market. Self-supporting means "that the income or donations from a given area will equal or exceed the expense of maintaining the program in that area. Most religious broadcasters expect a minimum ratio of two-to-one but aim for a ratio above three-to-one as a measurement guide for true success in a given area" (Lloyd, 1980:28).

However, certain assumptions about program content must be considered, since they make the results of these observations understandable. First, sponsors of television ministries, like sponsor of commercial programs, insist that the content be congruent with their advertising message system (Barnouw, 1978). Therefore, financial appeals indirectly reflect the values, priorities, and goals of the television ministries and the persona which each preacher attempts to cultivate. Second, the nature of a financial appeal is frequently related to other program elements. For example, a special ministerial project such as building a school would be scripted with interviews with school administrators. Musical themes would relate to the subject of the offerings, thus contributing to the appeal's emotional tone.

1. *Air Time Spent on Fundraising.* The amount of air time used to elicit financial support or viewer contact ranged from a low of 1.5 minutes an hour on the Jim Bakker show (of a filmed trip to Israel) to a high of 27.5 minutes on a thirty-minute Oral Roberts program devoted to fundraising for the City of Faith. For the sample as a whole, the median amount of air time used in fundraising was 8.8 minutes per thirty-minute segment.

Plate 14. Overview of the campus of Liberty Baptist College, Lynchburg, Virginia. Courtesy Old-Time Gospel Hour.

The average amount of air time used for fundraising by each preacher is presented in table 5. None of the preachers used less then 10 percent of air time for appeals, although three used less than ten minutes.

2. *Casting, or Who Asked for Funds.* In the forty-eight shows observed, 45 percent of the appeals were made by the preacher, 47 percent by an announcer, and 8 percent by a family member. Frequently, two individuals appeared in the same vignette, a format that is especially suitable for television (Esslen, 1982).

3. *Formats, or How the Request Was Structured.* During a revival meeting, passing the plate or making a free-will offering was part of the service. Television requests are structured in three different ways (table 6). A separate scripted segment similar to a commercial is used 43 percent of the time. This type of appeal is distinguishable from the rest of the program both by its separate context and by its placement in the show. In urban revivalism, the offering or fundraising generally preceded the main event or sermon. While the preacher may have actually exhorted the audience to contribute, this was a separate activity within the revival meeting (McLoughlin, 1959).

As a second approach, television preachers integrate funding or promotional appeals into the program itself 33 percent of the time. Falwell, in particular, has mastered this technique to such a great extent that it is at times difficult to draw a clear line between his preaching and

Table 5
Amount of Air Time Used by Television
Ministry for Financial Appeals

TV Ministry Relative Market Rank, 1981	Airtime Minutes	Average Minutes	Percentage Actual Airtime
1. Oral Roberts	30	9.3	31.0
2. Robert Schuller	60	7.2	12.0
3. Rex Humbard	30	12.8	42.6
4. Jimmy Swaggart	60	6.9	11.5
5. Jerry Falwell	60	13.8	23.0
6. Jim Bakker	60	13.8	23.0
7. Pat Robertson	90	14.2	15.7
8. James Robison	30	10.8	36.0

Table 6
Financial Appeal Format in Order of Relative Market Rank (May 1981)

| Preacher | Format of Appeal | | | |
	Spot Commercial	Integrated	Visual Display	Totals
Roberts	32%	42%	26%	100%
	(15)	(20)	(12)	(47)
Schuller	63%	37%	0	100%
	(19)	(11)	0	(30)
Humbard	39%	61%	0	100%
	(12)	(19)	0	(31)
Swaggart	96%	4%	0	100%
	(23)	(1)	0	(24)
Falwell	22%	74%	4%	100%
	(10)	(34)	(2)	(46)
Bakker	30%	54%	16%	100%
	(11)	(20)	(6)	(37)
Robertson	45%	21%	34%	100%
	(91)	(44)	(71)	(206)
Robison	42%	16%	42%	100%
Totals	(19)	(7)	(19)	(45)
	43%	33%	24%	100%
	(200)	(156)	(110)	(466)

his "promotionals." This observation was validated in Lloyd's study (Lloyd, 1980:23).

A third technique is the use of visual requests (24 percent) by running a telephone number or special message on the screen while the program is in progress. Together, the integrated and the visual requests were used 57 percent of the time. These are not comparable to any revivalistic practices. Neither are they acceptable practices for standard commercial advertising on television: according to industry guidelines, commercial advertising must be separate and distinct from program content (Lacey, 1978).

4. *Motivational Appeals.* There were reasons other than the contribution of funds for viewers to contact the ministry. Traditionally, revivalists relied on hellfire and brimstone to arouse fear in the individual, and the promise of salvation and redemption as a reward. The revivalist's job was to save souls and also raise enough cash to support his work (McLoughlin, 1955, 1959). But today's television revivalism is

expensive. The audience's financial support is essential for the continuation of the ministry. Consequently, appeals must be sufficiently
strong to elicit a letter or a telephone call.

As table 7 indicates, three basic motivational appeals were invoked.
These were categorized according to the beneficiary of the support:
(1) appeals to some personal need or service for the *viewer* (63
percent); (2) appeals to support the work of the television *ministry* (21
percent); and (3) appeals to help or influence *others* in the society (16
percent). The total number of financial appeals was 782. Although some
financial appeals were similar to those used by urban revivalist, others
were geared specifically to the unique demands of television broadcasting.

The most frequent appeals were directed at the personal need of the
viewer. These included such practices of popular religion as offering
souvenirs, instructional materials, personal help, or service. Pleas for
membership and continued watching are television-related appeals because they are based on the televangelists' attempt to build continuity
among their viewers. Memberships are particularly valuable technique
in obtaining financial support on a regular basis. Several of the pro-

Plate 15. Camera view of broadcast of "Old-Time Gospel Hour." Note the
similarity to Moody's gospel hall. Courtesy Old-Time Gospel Hour.

grams are know as clubs—the "700 Club" and the "PTL Club," for instance. Similarly, Rex Humbard asks viewers to become members of his "prayer key family." These devices are intended to motivate contributors to pledge regular amounts of money to a particular ministry. This regular flow of funds is, of course, important in the televangelist's organizational planning. It was not so important to the urban revivalist, who used anticipatory promotion to attract audiences to a one-time communal event, the revival meeting. Among the televangelists, there was variation in the amount or proportion of personal appeals which they used (see table 8). Oral Roberts made the least number of appeals (49 percent) for personal needs. This may be attributed to his ongoing emphasis, during this particular fundraising period, on the City of Faith Hospital and Research Center, a major project which required millions of dollars.

Financial appeals based on obligation to the ministry made up 21 percent of the total requests. Just as the urban revivalist asked for offerings to cover the cost of his revival campaign, so television preachers appeal for funds to cover the costs of air time. These analo-

Plate 16. Call-in segment of the "700 Club." Viewers call for help and to pledge their support. Photo courtesy of the Christian Broadcasting Network.

gous appeals, paying for air time and general support of the ministry, compose 28.6 percent of the ministry requests. Also included in these requests are two other categories, special ministry projects and a crisis appeal. These constitute 46.6 percent of the requests. Coded under these categories were requests for the City of Faith or improvements at Liberty Baptist College. A crisis appeal was some unexpected financial need, not based on a planned project, and usually caused by factors outside the control of the ministry. Jim Bakker, for example, had a financial crisis because of tax problems. A special plea for help with this problem would have been considered a special crisis appeal.

Table 7
Motivational Basis of Financial Appeals to Viewers

Motivational Basis		Percentage	Number
Appeals to Personal Need			
Souvenir, Memento		8.8	43
Instructional Material		18.2	89
Personal Help or Service		18.2	89
Membership		16.0	78
Job with TV Ministry		0.6	3
Professional or Educational Service		3.7	18
Trip with TV Ministry		2.0	10
Participate in Crusade		1.8	9
Continue to Watch Program		23.5	115
Demonstrate Love of God		1.6	8
Tell Us if Saved		5.7	28
	Total	100.0	490
Appeals to Obligation to Ministry			
Pay for Airtime		28.6	46
Special Project		37.9	61
Crisis (unexpected Financial)		8.7	14
Demonstrate General Support		24.8	40
	Total	100.0	161
Appeals to Christian Altruism*			
Evangelicalism		62.6	82
Charitable Works		17.6	23
Establish Moral Crusade		12.2	16
Support Political Activities		7.6	10
	Total	100.0	131

*Domestic and foreign combined

Table 8
Financial Appeals Invoked by Television Preachers

Television Preacher	Personal Need of Viewer	Ministerial Need	Christian Altruism	Totals
Roberts	49%	45%	6%	100%
	(35)	(32)	(4)	(71)
Schuller	63%	28%	9	100%
	(50)	(22)	(7)	(79)
Humbard	65%	22%	13%	100%
	(59)	(20)	(12)	(91)
Swaggart	51%	26%	23%	100%
	(27)	(14)	(12)	(52)
Falwell	51%	23%	26%	100%
	(76)	(35)	(38)	(149)
Bakker	66%	19%	15%	100%
	(43)	(12)	(10)	(65)
Robertson	71%	10%	19%	100%
	(145)	(21)	(39)	(205)
Robison	85%	8%	7%	100%
	(63)	(6)	(5)	(74)
Totals	63%	21%	16%	100%
	(498)	(162)	(127)	(787)

The last major category, requests to help or influence others altruism constituted percent of all appeals, making this the least used fundraising rationale. While altruism also played a role in the ministries of traditional evangelicals, it was not a major emphasis for them either. The interesting difference within this category is the introduction of new definitions of altruism. While altruism generally refers to charitable works (as contrasted with faith), this category also featured appeals to support political activities (7.6 percent) and to establish a moral crusade (12.2 percent), for example, a crusade against godless communism. These objectives are not part of the accepted social meaning of altruism and go beyond the religious obligation to help or assist the unfortunate.

While several of the techniques and appeals used by urban revivalists have been retained or adapted for television, many new ones have been added, so that the overall message has undergone not only a quantitative change but a qualitative one as well. Emphasis on appeals to the needs and motivations of individual viewers has changed the obligatory

Plate 17. Students on the campus of Liberty Baptist College. Courtesy Old-Time Gospel Hour.

and sacramental character of church giving. Today, each ministry has a carefully rationalized pattern of fundraising (Carlson, 1981; Lloyd, 1980). There is little doubt that these scripted promotional appeals are necessary to maintain the existing pattern of broadcasting and to provide revenues for the organizations.

The various leaders have all established their own style of fundraising, and they depend on their own credibility to generate financial support. This is not very different from the personal charisma and influence of prominent revivalists. The difference, however, lies in the fact that the offerings collected by urban revivalists were for the revival meeting itself, which was at least indirectly connected to community

Plate 18. Pat Robertson and Ben Kinchlow during a fund-raising telethon for the "700 Club." Photo courtesy of the Christian Broadcasting Network.

and church activity. This is not the case with televangelists. They script their personal fundraising messages to build committed audiences. Funds are used at each preacher's personal discretion to build his ministry or expand his television outreach without any meaningful accountability to the viewers who support him. Consequently, although fundraising appeals are still based on "old-time religion," their goals have been profoundly altered.

This close-up survey of fundraising techniques and appeals demonstrates that traditional revivalism and television imperatives have been combined into a new hybrid institution. While the religious norm of offerings has mixed with the broadcast norm of retaining audience support, the implicit obligation to meet viewers' religious or inspirational needs has been deemphasized. By count, admittedly a rough indicator, almost half of the fundraising appeals during the period studied can be traced to television-related functions rather than to religious functions. As a result, the hybrid institution of the electric ministry and its message have more of the special attributes of mass communication than of traditional popular religion.

Associated with these new characteristics are some underlying trends which should be of interest to both traditional mainline religious groups and political groups. First, the utilization and new allocation of resources by leaders of the electric church has fostered the development of new, multipurpose business organizations which produce these "religious" messages. Second, these religious messages, as we have seen in this chapter, have shifted their emphasis from inspirational concerns toward television-related matters. This indicates an underlying change in values for these producers. In particular, reciprocity between minister and audience has changed from sacred obligation to a system of personal rewards for the viewer. For these reasons, the electric church is not simply the recycling of one branch of the modernist/fundamentalist split: it represents a new message with the potential for new influence and effectiveness.

12

CONCLUSION

Authorities have always recognized that to control the public they must control information ... Leaders of democracies no less than medicine men, shamans, kings, and dictators are jealous of their power over ideas, as eager to control information as they are to control armies.

(Bagdikian, 1983:xiv)

THE ELECTRIC CHURCH HAS UTILIZED TELEVISION to send a particular, often sociopolitical message to millions of viewers. Its creation is the result of much more than a simple media switch by independent, Protestant evangelical ministers in an attempt to reach strayed and lapsed Christians with a gospel message. Rather, the electric church has developed as a significant and vigorous hybrid institution firmly entrenched as part of mass broadcasting in the United States. Moreover, its rapid expansion is turning it into an international broadcasting phenomenon as well. While the electric church traces its ancestry to nineteenth-century urban revivalism, what initially could be described as a media switch is now a complex social institution; although it may resemble its heterogeneous parents, televangelism is a different breed from either religion or television.

The electric church has grown to include approximately sixty nationally syndicated programs (some of which are broadcast seven days a week), five Christian cable networks, numerous religious-owned television and radio stations, and sophisticated television production facilities. One survey found that the top ten syndicated devotional programs reached an audience of "21% of all TV households" for at least six minutes (Clark and Virts, 1985). These vast holdings have enabled it to become a major sociopolitical movement expressing ultra-conservative political positions. Televangelists such as Jerry Falwell, Pat Robertson, and James Robison are acknowledged opinion leaders for the New Christian Right. No longer primarily in the business of saving souls, the electric church is engaged in "the battle of the mind."

The vigor and complexity of the electric church are much like the strength and vitality of a hybrid plant newly spawned from two divergent subspecies. In this instance, the progeny sprouted from the social structures, social relationships, and messages of urban revivalism, and from the profit-making, complex socio-technical production system of television. Let us briefly recall this process of creation before speculating on the future of the electric church.

Nineteenth-century urban revivalism, complete with its specialized roles, routinized traditions, and rituals of conversion, as well as its distinctive beliefs and religious values, provided a social structure ideally suited for the coming of mass broadcasting. As part of the dominant Protestant tradition, it was deeply embedded in popular culture at a time when America was evolving into an urbanized society—when the visible hand of management was replacing the invisible hand of the market in the nation's economic structure. A significant unintended consequence was the democratization of salvation. By the time mass broadcasting came into its own, urban revivalism was a stable, routinized, and rationally planned religious event. It had become an institution dedicated to evangelism with its own ethos, or values and beliefs, its own techniques and roles organized to achieve these ends. Characteristics that particularly suited it for mass broadcasting included its popular inspirational messages; mass audiences who supported it financially; its emphasis on preaching as the primary religious ritual; the revivalist's evangelical zeal; and the clear organizational mission that put it "in the business of saving souls by returning strayed or lapsed Christians to a renewed Christian life."

Especially critical to this process were the contributions of three revivalists: Finney, Moody, and Sunday. Finney's revivalism ethos of using appropriate means to stir religious enthusiasms made the use of purposive behavior the cornerstone of the revivalist's calling. Moody routinized the organization of revivalism and some of its rituals. He also applied business techniques to financial management and planning of revival meetings, including Moody attending to all the physical details involved in stirring up and maintaining interest within the community/

audience. Revivalism was pushed into popular religion not only by forcing a break from denominational control, but through preaching messages of Biblical inerrancy. Sunday, continuing this development, called himself a businessman for the Lord. He emphasized large-scale entertainment and streamlined his evangelical mission by concentrating on urban revivalism only. In this way, he differed from Finney and Moody, both of whom also set out to build educational organizations. Sunday defended his activities on a cost/benefit basis, documenting the large numbers of conversions which resulted from his efforts. Sunday left two clear legacies. First, he finished the process of urban revivalism, separating it from denominational Protestantism. Sunday drew his financial support and measures of success from the business world rather than the sacred realm. This left us with scientific management in the pulpit. Second, his dramatic preaching style, wedded to demagoguery, placed him in the cultural tradition of fundamentalism. What started with Finney's pragmatism was now joined with harsh biblical rhetoric, categorical patriotism, and anti-intellectualism.

The institution of urban revivalism was ready for television. Established was the ethos or belief that religious conversion can be stimulated and encouraged by conscious planning. The role of professional revivalist was central to translating this ethos of revivalism. The revivalist was an autonomous professional, building his own career, defining and enacting his goals as the situation required. His role was more akin to that of an entrepreneur than a churchman.

The television industry in the United States, while manifestly profit making, is part of the market-place primarily as an advertising medium. At the same time, it manufactures and transmits information, ideas, and cultural symbols. The leaders of the electric church have become expert in using the imperatives of television (standardized, formularized program formats; rationalized bureaucratic production systems) to market their programs.

It is important to recall that the history of religious broadcasting left a legacy of conflict. The inability of fundamentalists and independent religious groups to buy air time from the networks led to the formation of the National Religious Broadcasters. To this day, they monitor Federal Communication Commission activities and actively fight the networks. Today, they are entering an even newer phase of development by buying television stations (commercial and religious) and forming their own small networks.

Television is not a neutral medium. It is a complex technology that carries with it new systems of work and new tasks as well as changes in attitudes, values, and most importantly, ways of organizing reality for both program producers and receivers. This reorganization of communication by preachers constitutes a totally new construction of religious reality: suddenly, the religious message is being manufactured by a sophisticated, socio-technical work team that must respond to modern-day marketing demands in order to remain competitive in the religious marketplace. Content is distorted to fit the preexisting categories and formats of television; to meet economic requirements; and to translate into filmic images. This was demonstrated by the use of television formats and message changes by the leaders of the electric church.

The change in messages is the end result of rational decisions, impersonal rules associated with the imperatives of television. No longer driven by the charisma and zeal of the urban revivalist, these television programs are driven by the rational-legal authority of the television industry.

The heterogeneity of messages among leaders of the electric church is significant for a number of reasons. First, it dispels the perception by mainline church critics and station managers that all commercial religious programming is "old time religion" adapted for television. Second, the degree of divergence from old-time inspirational religion, as measured by message analysis, is so profound that clearly five of the eight electric church leaders operate in the socio-political realm. And, finally, variations in messages indicate some degree of heterogeneity in goals and objectives. While Swaggart, Schuller and Bakker appeared market driven, the remaining televangelists preached with concrete ideological objectives.

Preachers and Their Audiences

Program messages varied among the televangelists. If this product differentiation is a manifestation of the programmers' marketing strategy, then it would appear that different preachers speak to different audiences. Such a relationship was found in the 1981 data, and again by the Nielsen study commissioned by CBN in 1985.

In raising funds from their audiences the televangelists have been remarkably successful. In 1979 Marianni estimated a billion dollar enterprise for the electric church. Six years later, there is indication of continued financial success. The leaders of the electric church have bought additional air time and expanded the physical facilities of their various television ministries. Pat Robertson recently began building a graduate school of law and public policy as part of CBN University; Jim Bakker completed a hotel with penthouses as part of Heritage Village in Charlotte, North Carolina. It is in their fundraising appeals that the organizational priorities of the ministries are often reflected. The most frequent appeals are directed toward some personal need or service for the viewer; the second most frequent appeal is a direct request that viewers support the work of the television ministry (this included helping pay for building projects and organizational expenses); and finally, the third most common appeal was to help or influence others. These last appeals included solicitations to support moral or political activities of the television ministry. Regardless of the basis of appeals, funds received by the teleministries are outside any accountability, either to viewers or norms of religious stewardship. Generally speaking, evidence of how monies are spent is portrayed by camera shots of buildings, students, and campuses of the teleministers. This issue, however, does not speak to stewardship, that is, the proportion of "church" funds that should be spent on raising money. In the 1981 observations, almost half of all appeals were related to television expenses.

Today the television ministries are multipurpose business organizations dominated by television-related activities rather than inspirational, religious concerns. The reciprocity between minister and viewer has less to do with sacred obligation and more with personal rewards. The message is: "Support my ministry and I will send God's blessings."

In sum, systematically uncovering the structural basis of the electric church gives us a first step in building a theoretical framework. By placing the electric church into two institutional worlds, the worlds of urban revivalism and television, we can better understand both its success and the tension brought about by such crossbreeding.

The Significance of the Teleministries

Rationalization theory is a powerful tool in putting long-range historical processes into perspective. The overriding ethos of industrial society—a cost-accounting mentality and the urge to build and control institutions—helps explain both the ethos of urban revivalism and the ethos of religious television. The ethos of both reflects the historical periods in which they developed. The ethos of revivalism and its use of appropriate means fits into an era dominated by industrial capitalism; the ethos of religious television and the notion of God's technology fits neatly into the postindustrial era, in which technology will "solve" all our social problems. As part of the business and entrepreneurial tradition, televangelists are businessmen for the Lord. They are eager to seize available opportunities to sell the gospel through mass communications. They pursue their goals of winning souls and building teleministries without hesitation, never questioning the appropriateness of using television to do so. Neither are they encumbered by denominational deliberations. Rather, their concern is how to use television effectively. Schooled in pragmatism, televangelists know how to reach the individual Christian, offering hope and love to ameliorate fear and anxiety and, perhaps more importantly, offering membership into their television communities as a means of acknowledging the viewers' importance to them.

In addition to the use of any appropriate means to win souls, members of the electric church value the dynamics of a free-market economy in modern life, including competition for religious beliefs. They believe that the free market will recalibrate the economic system and the religious system and, because of this strongly held mindset, they claim to oppose federal government regulation and intervention. Despite their rejection of Darwinism, they equate successful competition with worthiness and confidently compete with other religious groups and organizations. One way they compete is by reaching out to those evangelicals who are nonaffiliated or disenchanted with their congregations. Another is by competing for the same, already established audience, as illustrated by Oral Roberts fighting to maintain his top-ranked position but losing to Jimmy Swaggart, or the fortunes of Rex Humbard and James Robison waning, but those of Pat Robertson and Jim Bakker rising.

Several related phenomena appear during such competition. First, the teleministries act like other institutions in similar situations. They try new program techniques. They hire new technical-professional staff. They contrive events to get their names in the papers and on television. They diversify their business activities by offering hotel facilities, special tours of their studios, schools for the children of viewers, and, in one case (Jim Bakker's Heritage Village), a theme park. In short, they engage in the business of staying in business, and, in the process, lose their uniqueness and mystery. Some would say they take on the organizational characterisitcs, staffing patterns, and goals and objectives of the secularized television industry. There remains, however, a major difference: the televangelists still cling to their calling to spread the gospel, and this distinguishes them from Adolph Coors or Ted Turner, businessmen first and evangelical fundamentalists second. Their missionary zeal remains an important factor in the operations of the teleministries and justifies their activities.

Religious broadcasting is institutionalized with a powerful ethos that keeps it dynamic. As Hadden and Swann (1981) predicted, there is the "potential to become a major force in shaping American culture." New documentation on the size of the religious television audience has reaffirmed this notion. It also corroborates the assumption that religious broadcasting is one aspect of a larger strategy of the New Christian Right.

The electric church has the potential to draw an even larger audience than it has today. We now know that its audience size is much larger than critics acknowledged. According to 1985 Nielsen data, 40 percent of 84.9 million television households watched one of the top ten religious programs at least once during February. This group may, in fact, regularly view religious television (Clark and Virts, 1985). This dispels any notion that religious television is a rural or Southern phenomenon. More accurately it is a national phenomenon.

Who watches religious television? While women over fifty still compose the largest audience segments, ther are also large proportions of men in the audience. The programs of Jimmy Swaggart and Jerry Falwall "attract the smallest number of women (43% each)" (Clark and Virts, 1985:20). Interestingly, the programs of Jerry Falwell and Pat Robertson "are more likely to attract younger men" (Clark and Virts:21). Children compose thirty percent of Falwell's audience. There is no question that the electric church audience is more diverse than the original Nielsen and Arbitron data revealed. This confirms the assumption that "different programs attract different types of audiences" (Clark and Virts:21).

In spite of these burgeoning figures, which suggest that, for the time being, the electric church can be expected to become an even stronger societal force, there are inherent limits to its growth which can eventually slow down its spread. Some of these limitations are external and beyond its control; other limitations are internal and could be controlled.

One external factor is demographics. It is true that the population is aging, but there is little to suggest that these individuals will become electric church viewers. A factor more predictive of electric church expansion is conservative church membership. Audience survey data indicate that many viewers are already members of ultraconservative evangelical churches. Many are born-again Christians. In other words, the audience is tuning in to reinforce a religiosity it already holds. Along with the growth of the conservative churches, there has been an expansion of the conservative infrastructure, primarily through its schools and other community activities. As long as conservative church membership continues to grow, audience potential will exist.

Clearly the relationship between the preacher and the audience is very different from that in commercial television. Viewers may regularly watch a particular program and buy the sponsor's products, but this is a transient commitment and must be continually reinforced. For many viewers of religious television, the commitment extends beyond merely watching the program to actually participating in the services and activities of the ministry. Many of the teleministries offer memberships to their viewers as part of their process of audience building.

If, however, the television audience remains relatively stable, competition among televangelists is likely to become even more fierce than it is now. As noted earlier, the top eight televangelists account for most of the market. Unabated, such a competitive struggle raises the possibility that internal factors—poor management, overexpansion, scandal or fraud, or dissension—might force some of these televangelists out of the picture.

On the other hand, of course, a stable audience size is a stable contribution base. Most reports of audience contributions indicate that 20 percent of viewers contribute funds and that the average contribution is $20 per viewer. Unfortunately, these studies do not indicate if this is a yearly total. If we calculate this very low estimate based on the CBN data, the top programs receive $67,920,000 annually. While this is enormous revenue, there is no available data on expenditures. Consider, though, if stability does not produce financial growth: this puts economic pressure on the teleministries to expand and diversify their services and make other organizational changes in response to market competition.

There are other external factors which could limit the growth of the electric church. As the broadcast industry faces a proliferation of new technology—from home videocassette recorders to narrowcast to low-frequency channels—there will be industry-wide competition for the viewing public. Commercial television has been concerned about this ever since television viewing in general began to decline. Still, a new stage of technological development is yet to come through the convergence of technologies, combining several media for new uses.

Television, telephone and computer, for example, could be used for interactive communications. Already many legal questions regarding this combination of delivery and content medium have been raised, primarily because of the two different regulatory domains involved, Regardless, as these competing technologies offer innovative means of reaching people, the electric church will seize them as new means to stir religious enthusiasm.

While new technology opens up opportunities for religious broadcasters, it could also lead to a saturation of the religious market. To protect their interests, televangelists are developing market segmentation strategies. They are developing programs targeted to the black population, to young people, or to Hispanics, for example. These groups, along with many other special populations, provide new opportunities for televangelists to carry their message beyond their traditional audience base. One of the most significant market segmentation strategies took place in 1981 when CBN introduced its news-magazine format, an innovation made specifically to attract non-Christian viewers. Activities of this kind surely indicate that while we cannot predict continued expansion of the electric church, we can anticipate a permanent and aggressive presence.

The Sacred and the Profane

Weber identified inner-worldly and other-worldly tensions as being similar to what Durkheim described as the sacred and the profane. The sacred comprises those "things set apart and forbidden." A religion, according to Durkheim, is a unified system of beliefs and practices associated with these sacred things. These beliefs and practices function to unify the moral community or the social group into what we call a church (Durkheim, 1951). Part of the difficulty in assessing the electric church, and some of the conflict surrounding it, can be traced to an erosion of boundaries between sacred and profane. This is evident on many levels.

Television broadcasting, according to televangelists, is a God-given gift. Yet television is the epitome of the secular life, a marketing medium for consumer products and a showplace for glamorous celebrities and stars. Televangelists rail against it as a source of godlessness, pornography, licentiousness, and mind control, but the inescapable fact is that they are part of the television world. Television techniques have enabled them to succeed. This dichotomy clearly presents dilemmas and internal conflicts. For one thing, broadcasting, with its highly technical and rapidly changing technology, is a multimillion-dollar industry. Today, there are television dishes and satellites for relays, complex control boards for instant editing of sound and camera shots, and portable video cameras for on-the-spot transmission. The equipment is costly and expensive to operate. In addition, technical and marketing staff must be employed. While operational and organizational streamlining can realize some savings, these are generally offset by high costs of equipment and air time. Building larger audiences is the logical way of making the process cost-effective, but, as illustrated previously, this requires modification of formats and messages.

Proud as it is of its expansion and success, the electric church is aware of tensions between its sacred and secular goals. Armstrong (1985) sees the reconciliation of these goals as the single most difficult challenge for National Religious Broadcasters (NRB). In the meantime, obviously pleased that charges of competition with local churches have been disproved by the Annenberg study, at least for NRB members, Armstrong continues to urge religious broadcasters to use technical opportunities to spread the gospel.

The Annenberg study, however, did little to change the minds of critics of the electric church. The use of television for religious purposes remains ancillary to the critics' work. Television is clearly in the realm of the profane.

Another aspect of the tension between sacred and profane is manifested in the disparity between the ethos of television professionals and the ethos of religious professionals within the electric church. Religious broadcasters are not merely using the tools of the industry, but are imbued with the professionalism of broadcasters in their day to day activities. Today, they are acquiring and operating a full range of broadcasting facilities, commercial stations, cable networks, and production facilities. Some are even operating communication schools. This is evidence of their commitment to the professional world of broadcasting. These various entities are loosely connected by the nearly 1200 memberships in the NRB (1986). The NRB services its members with information and professional standards and serves as a forum for new technology and ideas. It also represents members before the Federal Communications Commission and in legislative matters. Clearly, this is a mature professional broadcasting group.

Members of the electric church claim to be speaking the gospel. They alone have the Christian outlook. In effect, the FCC supports this literal reading of their activities by interpreting regulations to permit them to continue to function as religious organizations. This categorical interpretation of FCC regulations ignores the religious hegemony of the electric church. This makes the fairness doctrine, which requires broadcasters to "provide reasonable opportunity for the presentation of contrasting viewpoints," not relevant for this type of programming. Meanwhile, mainline religions, dependent on sustaining air time, are in the same position as were evangelicals in the early days of broadcasting. Faced with economic and denominational barriers, they are prevented from broadcasting as much as they would like to.

Up to the present, FCC policy has had a direct impact on the expansion of religious broadcasting. By continuing to classify any religious organization, regardless of the political content of its message or the commercial nature of related enterprises, as religious-nonprofit, the FCC is subsidizing the growth of the electric church (Lacey, 1978). This means that any monies contributed to the teleministries are tax-free. Admittedly, many religious organizations thrive under these tax laws; they would hardly want to take issue against other other religious organizations, including the Unification Church, since this would jeopardize their own finances.

Regulatory law is ultimately based on a social norms, which are modified over time. Therefore, we cannot assume that the law is inviolate or immutable. The issue raised here, in relation to the electric church, is whether some of it practices and profit-making aspects are within the realm of the sacred.

While the electric church's nonprofit status augments its financial growth, there is a still more significant problem. Television has great symbolic importance. The ability to make television such an effective institutional resource enhances the position of the electric church in society. In the process of expanding its audiences and building its teleministries, the electric church has acquired legitimacy and social status. Seen in this perspective, the subsidization of the electric church is a social problem with serious ramifications, and a much larger question than the issue of financial accountability within individual television ministries. By redefining religious-institutional goals and using mass broadcasting to meet these goals, there is no question that the electric church has been building its presence in broadcasting as part of a larger social movement. In this instance, the joining of urban revivalism and television has institutionalized the New Christian Right.

Such institutionalization is not new in our culture. Education, health care, and police protection are examples of social functions that have undergone transformations and developed permanent organizations. Significantly, in the process of institutionalization each of these functions was removed from community and family control and placed under bureaucratic control. This trend has been a powerful and pervasive aspect of postindustrial society. Part of the social control and power that these institutions wield derives from their relative stability and permanence. Some of their power is based on their hierarchical position in society. The hybrid electric church, which includes the New Christian Right, derives much of its vigor from its affiliation with television, the premier mass-communications medium. As a thriving member of the television industry, the electric church has acquired power, status, and legitimacy. These attributes enchance and magnify its messages.

There is an inherent tension here. The ideology of the New Christian Right supports privatization of social functions and opposes government and institutional controls. Yet it is the building of institutional infrastructures which, in large measure, enables it to grow.

The Future of the Electric Church

Few would quarrel with the notion that the leaders of the electric church have been using television as a means of social control, of transmitting their own ideology. Signs of the larger social movement and its agenda are visible everywhere. The Christian Broadcast Network sees its goal as providing alternative broadcasting. The recent attempted takeover of CBS was part of this objective. In addition, coalitions have been established between leaders of the electric church and leaders of political groups. The Moral Majority is only one example of this. These activites are all part of a coherent, multi-purpose plan. These coalitions contribute to the centralization of ideas and resources. They also provide continuity and control for the social movement. CBN audience data clearly indicate that many millions of television households watch the top ten religious programs. While we do not know whether, in fact, these viewers are followers in the same social movement, CBN claims, "these programs clearly have the potential of influencing the thinking and behavior of the American public in various ways . . . Many of these programs touch on topics such as marriage, education, news, politics and public policy, psychology, medicine and others considered to be outside the rather narrow program category thought of by many as 'religious broadcasting.' It may be difficult to find evidence that these programs influence what viewers think, but it is clear, these programs are setting an agenda of what viewers will think about" (Clark and Virts, 1985:23).

We are now in an era when religious television has the power—and, so the televangelists believe, the responsibility—to control the agenda for what many people discuss and argue in the public domain. The electric church in general, and the leading televangelists in particular, have arrogated to themselves this responsibility, perhaps in an attempt to fill the void left by the weakening of our country's democratic values and ideals. But a country dominated by televangelism would be unrecognizable to the Founding Fathers, who envisioned religion as personal and spiritual, not social and political. No particular variety of religion was intended to control the political agenda, to set the community's moral tone, or to judge who are the true believers and members of our society. But this is precisely the objective of the electric church.

APPENDIXES
BIBLIOGRAPHY
INDEX

Appendix A
RESEARCH STRATEGY AND METHODOLOGY

Research Strategy

According to Mills, personal observational skills with historical perspective and a sociological imagination are prerequisites for "serious social observation" (Mills, 1972:6). Methods are to be adapted to the exigencies of the problem at hand. Quality research "is based on ideas and disciplined by fact" (Mills, 1972:7). With these words in mind, I decided on a research strategy that combined a variety of investigative approaches and techniques. One strategy used historical analysis to account for the development of the electric church and to grasp "history and biography and the relations between the two within society" (Mills, 1972:6). The other strategy involved collecting and analyzing data to study current practices of the electric church through their actual programs. By understanding both historical and contemporary practice, we can see that in this case, the past and present are mutually confirmatory and explanatory. We can understand "what is going on in the world" (Mills, 1972:7).

A brief narrative of the stages of field work details the research used here. Stage one, an initial immersion in the topic, served to answer basic descriptive questions about the electric church. During this period, literally hundreds of hours of religious broadcasts were watched and the varieties of programming categorized and analyzed. The initial attempt at program content analysis used the coding categories for inspirational literature designed by Schneider and Dornbusch (1958) in *Popular Religion*, as well as categories developed specifically for the context of television.

Further investigation during this period included interviewing key informants: Reverend Mason McGuinness of the Meadville-Lombard Theological School of the University of Chicago; Steve Sewell, Federal Communications Commission; and Richard Ostrander of the OZMA Broadcast Sales Company. They were interviewed to help formulate the research questions.

During Stage two, I studied techniques of content analysis at the Annenberg School of Communication at the University of Pennsylvania. I also conducted additional field interviews with the following persons: Everette Parker, United Church of Christ; Professor Barry Cole, Annenberg School of Communications; and Reverend Thea Jones, a television revivalist who broadcasts in the Philadelphia area. In addition, I attended three revival meetings conducted in the area: one at the Bryn Mawr Gospel Hall, another at the Delaware County Baptist Church in Pilgrim Gardens, and an Ernest Angeley Crusade at the Civic Center.

During Stage three, I developed my coding categories for collection of data and conducted further field interviews—"host verifications" for measures of validity. "Credibility may be established with some audiences by showing or simply stating that at least the major propositions were tested or checked against the experiences and understanding of the hosts" (Schatzman and Strauss, 1973:134). As a research strategy to study the electric church, this field perspective required using a variety of methodological techniques, no one of which was complete in and of itself, but all of which contributed to the composite picture of the electric church. The logic of this design is inductive, in accordance with the procedures described by Glaser and Strauss (1967) and Schatzman and Strauss (1973). This composite and inductive method meets the criteria for systematic observation.

> The observer of human events listens to how persons in given situations present to themselves and to others (including the naturalist) the "realities" and contexts of their lives. Meanwhile, he correlates what he himself sees with what he hears from these persons who stand in different relationships to each other and to the whole situation. The observer is then able to develop an abstract, logical, and empirically grounded representation of the

observed situation.... His task requires distinctive and flexible strategies to maximize discovery in the situation—a situation special in many ways but particularly in that the observer is an outsider in an otherwise "inside world." (Schatzman and Strauss 1973:13)

At the end of my stages one and two, the clear fact emerged that the message system of the televangelists had not been empirically studied (Hadden, 1980). From this gap in our sociological investigations, I formulated my guiding research question: Is the electric church the result of a media switch or is it a new institution?

Content Analysis Procedures

Content analysis is a systematic technique used by social scientists to analyze many forms of communication. Communication content is summarized into a set of categories determined by the research objectives. It is basically an observational technique and can be operationalized for many types of communications (Budd et al., 1967: 2; Krippendorff, 1980; Lazarsfeld and Barton, 1951; Markoff et al., 1974).

Berelson's seminal definition of content analysis set the parameter of the research technique as an "objective, systematic, and quantitative description of manifest content of communication" (in Budd et al., 1967:3). Much communication research is merely a recording of manifest content. Traditionally, the sociologist using content analysis is concerned with larger questions, perhaps regarding the origins or production of communication or the effects of communication; in other words, why and how content is sent. What can we learn about communication behavior and its effects (cf. Merton, 1946:493–584)? For a study of communication as a social act or form of behavior, the actual messages under study are conceptualized as indices of social action. This, I hardly need mention, is within traditional sociological analysis—Weber, Marx, and Mannheim examined communication as aspects of behavior.

In modern sociological research, content analysis and message system analysis, while within the large sociological tradition, are specific research methodologies, empirically based and subject to canons of scientific measurement which have evolved primarily from a body of communication studies (Holsti, 1969; Krippendorff, 1980). At the same time, sociological use of content analysis, while adhering to the rigors of scientific measurement, must conceptualize data categories that are rooted in sociological theory: the quality of the research process is ultimately assessed on the degree of theoretical integration with data collection techniques (Markoff, 1974; Mills, 1972). Content or message analysis per se, to use Gerbner's terminology, is not equated with scientific research; it must meet the prevailing standards of conceptualization for data collection and minimization of investigator bias as well as connect the study to the tradition of sociology.

Despite this cautionary introduction, content analysis of television shows recommends itself as an important and useful technique for this study for several compelling reasons. First, it is an unobtrusive measure (Webb, 1966) and readily lends itself to systematic observations while controlling or eliminating experimenter bias. Second, the preachers' programs constitute a major record of their behaviors and, as such, are major areas for inquiry and analysis. In organizational terms, the programs are critical events for the ministry and represent the manifest message of the preacher. Third, the programs as data were readily available through the use of video recording equipment. Although the use of video equipment and coders is an expensive research procedure, the relative certainty of obtaining video files compensates for the costs.

And finally, a study of religious programs and documentation of their messages was, in my opinion, a logical first step toward a sociological understanding of the electric church. This exploratory research objective is based on the assumption that changes in messages reflect changes in the institutions producing these messages.

The procedural or methodological steps for message system analysis are as follows: (1) develop the coding categories and a coding instrument that operationalizes specific research concepts; (2) select and train coders (or observers) to collect data; (3) select the sample; (4) collect data on coding instruments; and (5) tabulate and analyze data (Holsti, 1969; Krippendorff, 1980).

The preliminary work for category development began in the spring of 1979. By observing religious programs of all varieties, I determined the complete range of behavioral categories. The pretesting phase, using Schneider and Dornbusch's coding scheme, clearly pointed out the need to focus the research instrument on a relatively limited number of categories. Contrary to an analysis of written materials, it is impossible to code all elements in a television program because more than sentences or thoughts constitute communication—sounds, movements, placement, proportion, and visual images are all part of the message, and some determinations have to be made as to what parts of the program will be coded and how this will be done.

Developing the categories and instruments to operationalize research concepts. As in any research process, bridging the gap between abstract theoretical categories and observations of behavior is an imperfect joining at best. In this case, there were no precedents or models to provide comparative categories. There were, however, comparisons to be made between the electric church and urban revivalism, the ideal type of which is detailed in chapter 7. At the same time, television content analysis had to be context-specific, that is, categories had to be based on observable features of each program, regardless of format. All the selected programs had a preacher; they often used guests; the preacher delivered a message; and all had some fundraising activity. These elements were the basis for program observations. The sociological questions were derived from the preacher's role performance and message. What was the preacher's role in the program? What was the main content of the message, and were there significant differences or variations among the preachers in their roles and their messages? If so, what explained or accounted for these differences? Beharrell, 1976: 42, Holsti, 1969; Lazarsfeld and Barton, 1951).

The development of the coding instrument for recording observations was the next operation. This procedure consisted of creating increasingly smaller and smaller data categories to record observations. These categories had to be specific, contextual, feasible, logical, and mutually exclusive and exhaustive (Schultz, 1958).

At the same time, categories had to be precise and specific enough to minimize coder judgment. This was accomplished with the data sheets, intensive coder training, and a system of logical or chronological categories which were exhaustive and which contained examples in parentheses (Lazarsfeld and Barton, 1951). A complete set of data sheets appears in appendix B. Table 9 presents the conceptualization process in outline form.

The development of the coding instrument is a difficult process. The actual use of the instrument by the coders proved to be the most effective way to hasten the process and determine its usefulness (Milke, 1980).

Selection and training of coders. Two uniquely qualified coders were selected to observe the video tapes. Both were students in cognitive areas that utilized abstract thinking and manipulation of logic and symbols. One coder was a doctoral student in philosophy at Bryn Mawr College, and the other an undergraduate student majoring in classics at Haverford. Neither student was personally involved in politics or in practicing his religion. Either activity would have interfered with their ability to observe the programs objectively. Throughout the project they remained detached viewers, while maintaining interest and commitment to the project (Gottschalk et al., 1969).

Table 9

Televangelists' Message System Concepts Operationalized for Coding Observations

Sociological Concept	Major Category for Observation	Operationalization
1. Church offerings	Requests to viewers to contact ministry	*Techniques* 1. Amount of time number 2. Casting—who makes request 3. How/format used *Motivational Appeals* 1. Personal need of viewer 2. Minister's need 3. Christian altruism
2. Witnessing	Use of Guests	*Techniques* 1. Number used *How Used* 1. Religious 2. Secular

3. Role Enactment	Role of Preacher	*Techniques*
		1. *Source of legitimacy*
		  a. Source of calling
		  b. Rationale to followers
		  c. Refers to significant others—
		     family, celebrities
		2. *Tasks on program*
		3. *Style of preaching*

4. Preacher's Message	Message Content	*Religious Beliefs* Path to salvation Guide to Christian life Security Type of millenarianism
	Emphasis on moral and social conditions	*Political Beliefs and Issues* *Sources* *Remedies* of Society's problems

A three-week training period served two main purposes. First, it taught the coders how to collect the data, and second, it served to complete the development of the coding instrument. At the beginning of the training process, each coder was provided with a brief coder's manual with basic information on the project and definitions of major terms (see appendix B). The coders also familiarized themselves with the eight programs during this period. A file of demonstration tapes was set aside for this purpose. A set of coding sheets was used to begin the actual learning process. Observed behaviors were matched with categories. This was structured in an orderly manner: one concept was operationalized at a time. For example, all the categories for "requests to viewers" were completely developed before the next set ("use of guests") was operationalized. In this manner, exhaustive categories were developed and definitional problems were resolved before starting a new set of observations and category development.

At the end of each training session, data sheets were revised to incorporate changes. Logical errors and ambiguities were eliminated. Examples were added to eliminate or minimize coder decisions and to supplant the use of a coder manual. The physical layout of the data sheets was streamlined for easy reading and recording. One way of doing this was to set out the categories and the pages to conform to program development, if possible. By the end of three weeks, the final data set was polished for use, and data collection could proceed.

One television show, one airing of a program, constituted a unit of analysis. Television observation and coding is extremely tedious and very complex. In order to maximize coder reliability, work periods were confined to no more than four hours. The coders observed together, but they scored individual data sets, one per program. They did, however, use one stopwatch to time "requests to viewers" and alternated this job between themselves. When the variable coding was transferred to the computer, scores were randomly selected from the two sets of data sheets. This was another safeguard for reliability.

Intercoder reliability was checked both after the training period and upon completion of the data collection period. Agreement was .96 for all data sheets, with the exception of categories "preacher style" where agreement was only .84 (Holsti, 1969). Coding analysis revealed that this set of categories was perceived as judgmental and subjective. This same problem was noted in Holsti (1969).

Reliability and validity in using content analysis are heightened through specific techniques for improving intercoder reliability and through criteria for category development (Holsti, 1969). Intercoder reliability seeks to establish procedures to ensure that different coders secure the same results when they apply the same set of categories to the same material. Careful training procedures ensure replication in data collection, and reliability can be measured for different parts of the coding process. The percentage of agreement between coders will vary directly with the specificity of the category. This indeed was the experience in this project. Measures of fundraising time, which was measured with a stopwatch, and the frequency of fundraising appeals were more reliable than measures of preaching style.

Validity in a descriptive study can be assessed by face or content validity (Holsti, 1969). The consistency with other evidence and comparison of findings to external data are adequate techniques by which the researcher may assess face validity. If the instrument measures what it is intended to measure, with little ambiguity, face validity is ascertained. Care in determining frequency of occurrence is important in this process. By the use of category development, face validity is also enhanced. The general standard is that the empirical evidence must be sufficiently clear so that competent judges can agree; for this reason, two coders were used for the duration of the data collection period. Other techniques to enhance face validity are instrument design and coder training, which have already been explained. These include such precautions as logical correctness, explicit definitions and examples, use of dichotomies, decision trees, training, pretesting of the instrument, adaptation to the structure of the situation, congruence with the syntax of television, and adaptation to the actor's frame of reference. Judicious and alternative selection of indicators together with logical sequencing of categories all enhance validity, according to Berelson (1952) and Schutz (1958). As indicated in my narrative, these issues were all addressed in my careful procedures.

Sample design. This study is limited to the programs of the leaders of the electric church. In 1981, Nielsen ratings identified sixty-five nationally syndicated devotional programs and ranked them by order of audience size. Eight preachers from this ranking were identified as pacesetters or leaders in the electric church: Oral Roberts, Robert Schuller, Rex Humbard, Jimmy Swaggart, Jerry Falwell, James Robison, Jim Bakker, and Pat Robertson. These eight have maintained relatively large shares of the local devotional market up to 1985 and established national reputations as television preachers. Although these ministries were selected by 1981 data, subsequent interviews with Ben Armstrong and Peggy George (Oral Roberts' marketing director) confirmed the initial judgment that these are the leaders of the electric ministry. Billy Graham, while closely associated with the electric church and its development, is not part of the sample here because his programs are specials; air time is purchased throughout the year as the need arises. Graham does not produce a weekly show.

The programs studied are all broadcast on a weekly basis, except for Jim Bakker's "PTL Club" and Pat Robertson's "700 Club," which are broadcast seven days a week. The sample programs were selected from shows aired in Philadelphia between May 2 and July 19, 1981. The television ministries share the following characteristics: (1) they are led by an evangelical preacher; (2) the program buys broadcasting time; and (3) the program is rated by Nielsen in the category of nationally syndicated devotional.

Appendix B

CODING CATEGORIES USED IN CONTENT ANALYSIS

**Definitions of Terms for Use by the Coders:
TV Ministries' Data Sheets**

Requests to Viewers. In church practice, offerings and tithing are obligations by which the member contributes a portion of his or her income for the purpose of supporting both clergyman and church property. This obligation rests on both divine law and natural law. Requests for "offerings" or financial contributions for TV ministries occur in many forms. For this study, identify any means which encourage viewers to contact, respond, write, or call the ministry as "requests to viewer." For example, this would include any appeal to viewers for letters, money, or telephone calls, or generalized solicitation of viewer support regardless of the anticipated viewer action.

Format refers to the style or structure of offering request. Television uses visual and verbal messages. Phone numbers on screen may be one format used. Count phone numbers flashed, if not part of spot advertisement segment.

Minister's special project. Many ministries plan and develop special projects or events for their ministry. These projects are directly connected to the ministry, implemented by them, and often originate at the site of the broadcast facility.

Christian altruism refers to projects or goals directed to unfortunate others such as refugees, the unchurched in Germany, drug addicts, war victims, and so forth.

Evangelicalism. Defined as propagation of Christian faith among non-Christian people. Note that non-Christian in this context refers to individuals who have not had a born-again experience. Reference to this activity generally indicates use of broadcasting among specific groups of people, a crusade or evangelical revival meeting, sending a missionary to an area, building a church or church school. An evangelicalist is a traveling missionary.

Charitable works refers to those activities which help others in their distress, such as helping refugees resettle, providing food, medical care, and so on.

Establish moral crusade refers to a specific attempt to change or influence values, behaviors, or beliefs of non-Christian groups, but not directly related to spreading the gospel, for example changing school curriculum, mounting antipornography drive, antialcoholism, antismoking, and so forth.

Support political activities. This includes direct attempts to influence legislation, to influence voting, or party platform.

Program format. Each program has a format or style which is identifiable and associated with a particular TV ministry. Of particular interest to this study are two roles, the preacher (major) and the guest.

Preacher characteristics specific to preaching. This is a judgment on your part, and if possible, make the decision within the context of the particular show being coded. Under the category of plainness of speech, base your decision on vocabulary selection and ease of comprehension.

Guests. Many programs use guests. Observations of characteristics and their contribution to the program format are of interest. Many guests express their personal religious convictions and conversion experience. This church ritual is called witnessing and may include acknowledgment of sin and confession of faith. Listen to the story to determine life before conversion (problem statement), the mechanism of conversion (to what is conversion attributed), and what happened after conversion (changes, if any). If guest tells about someone else's religious experience, that is, a second-hand account of witnessing, code as a witnessing story and indicate context.

Comments. Any comments or additional information may be noted on sheets. Make sure all categories are filled out and completed. Check top of sheets also.

Figure 3. Data Sheet for Requests to Viewers

DATA SHEET: TV MINISTRIES
PROGRAM ID _____ FILE # _____ CODER _____

1 SUBJECT: REQUESTS TO VIEWERS (FOR MONEY, LETTERS, CALLS, SUPPORT)

1. QUANTITY OF REQUESTS
   a. estimated time (stopwatch) _____
   b. total number of requests _____ = _____
2. CASTING: role making request
   a. preacher _____
   b. family member _____
   c. announcer _____

3. TYPE/FORMAT OF REQUEST
   a. _____ spot (segment similar to ad; often filmed, not part of progam content)
   b. _____ integrated (part of program content, may be announce-ment, part of sermon, or developed as special segment)
   c. _____ phone numbers (flashed on screen, not part of spot)
   d. _____ other, specify

4. REASONS FOR VIEWER TO CONTACT TV MINISTRY

(note if mentioned, & frequency)

a. for viewer's personal use/needs:

1 _____ souvenir, memento, memorial (gift, pin, jewelry, etc.)
2 _____ instructional material (copy of sermon, book, Bible, newsletter, magazine, etc.)
3 _____ personal help or service (prayer, counselling)
4 _____ membership (in tv ministry, pledge)
5 _____ job with tv ministry
6 _____ professional or educational service
7 _____ trip with tv ministry
8 _____ participate in crusade
9 _____ continue to watch program
10 _____ demonstrate love of God
11 _____ tell us if Saved (relate personal religious experience, call if healed)
12 _____ other (specify)

TOTAL a = _____

b. for minister's use/needs:

1 _____ pay for air time (continuation)
2 _____ pay for air time (expansion)
　　　　 USA　　　　OUTSIDE USA
3 _____ SPECIAL PROJECT: _____
　　　　 (on site bldg. special event, directly related to ministry)
4 _____ CRISIS (unexpected financial need, not based on own plans, factors outside their control)
5 _____ demonstrate general support of our tv ministry
6 _____ other _____

c. for Christian Altruism (or influencing others)

| | OUTSIDE | | |
USA	USA	TO USE FOR	
1		Evangelicalism (spread Gospel)	
2		charitable *works* (feed, care for, educate, cloth others, etc.)	
3		establish moral crusade (to influence norms & values of others, establish Christian leadership)	
4		support political activities	

Figure 4. Data Sheet for Use of Guests

DATA SHEET: TV MINISTRIES
PROGRAM ID _____ FILE # _____ CODER _____   2 SUBJECT: USE OF GUESTS

1. GUEST ID & COUNT
   a. Used on program yes_____ no_____
   b. Number used = _____
2. MAIN CONTRIBUTION OF GUEST
   a. Religious task (e.g., musical, Bible teaching, witnessing, preaching,
      religious announcement) _____
   b. Secular task (contributes advice, guide for living, information)
      _____
   c. TOPIC: _____

3. Characteristics:
   a. name _____   e. Note other characteristics
   b. occupation _____   _____
   c. ethnic id _____   f. male_____ female_____
   d. age +65_____ +30_____   white_____ black_____
      +19_____ youth_____   other_____
4. Interviews guest: yes_____ no_____. If yes,
5. Relates: a. personal religious experience
               (testimony) _____
            b. speaks only on expertise _____
            (If 5a, use Part II)

PART II: IF INTERVIEWED ABOUT RELIGIOUS EXPERIENCE

6. Prior circumstances to religious event indicate need for:
   a. physical health _____
   b. mental health _____
   c. spiritual health _____
   d. financial help _____
   e. social problem (not personal, cause attributed to society) _____
   f. other _____

7. Specificity of religious event:
   a. specific event _____
   b. happened over time _____
   c. vague _____

8. Nature of religious experience or event which contributed to solution of problem:
   a. born again experience _____
   b. divine intervention _____
   c. help from tv ministry _____
   d. help from other sources _____
   e. personal efforts (behavior changes after religious event) _____
   f. other _____

9. Changes after religious event:
   a. physical healing _____
   b. mental healing _____
   c. spiritual healing (e.g., found peace of mind, found meaning, focus to life) _____
   d. financial healing (prosperity, solved financial crisis) _____
   e. assured of Salvation (removed all doubts) _____
   f. surrender to God (removed need to make decisions) _____
   g. became new person (gained control of own life, new sense of self-worth) _____
   h. life in general is better (relations with family, friends improved) _____
   i. expect a miracle (self) _____
   j. expect a victory (world) _____
   k. other _____

Figure 5. Data Sheet for Preachers

DATA SHEET: TV MINISTRIES

PROGRAM ID _____ FILE # _____ CODER _____   SUBJECT: PREACHER

1. Minister attributes his calling to:

   a. divine instruction (personally called by God; instrument for God & his will; personal revelation; or derived from word of God, i.e., Bible)_____

   b. special powers from divine source (gift of healing, distributor of divine goods)_____

   c. trained, educated for job_____

   d. as a model Christian (wants to be example to others, wants others to be Saved, as happy as he is)_____

   e. other_____

3. SUBJECT: PREACHER

2. Rationale for following preacher (if both, note highest emphasis, lowest)

   a. obligation, viewer has ethical duty to obey his authority_____

   b. in self-interest for viewer (means for personal reward/punishment)

3. Refers to famous or highly placed people

   (name:) yes _____ no _____

4. Family:

   uses family on program   yes _____ no _____

   refers to family on program   yes _____ no _____

5. *Preachers role on program & style of preaching*

Estimate amount of emphasis given to following segments. Indicate High (largest amount of time); moderate (smaller amount of time); and low (minimal time); not present (0).

a. delivers sermon _____
b. announcements _____

c. m.c. (introduces other segments) _____
d. prays _____

e. informs & teaches _____
f. interviews others _____

6. Style of preaching (check applicable descriptions)

a. traditional homily with 4 parts: Bible reading, message, explanation & application

b. style relies on reason, uses well-structured message with parts connected & apt. examples _____

c. appears spontaneous & impromptu, conveys familiarity with listener _____

d. uses strong emotional & sentimental appeals such as fear, guilt, hope to excite psychological/ emotional response _____

e. delivery is formal _____

f. delivery is dramatic _____

g. conveys disapproval to listeners _____

h. presentation is dogmatic, positive in manner & judgments _____

i. is sympathetic to others & willing to listen to other views _____

j. is matter of fact, businesslike in manner

k. is warm and shows affection to others

l. plainness of speech provides instant comprehension _____

m. builds anxiety into presentation (often used to create motivation in listener) _____

DATA SHEET: TV MINISTRIES
PROGRAM ID _____ FILE # _____ CODER _____   5   SUBJECT: PREACHER CONTENT OF MESSAGE CONT.

Figure 6. Data Sheet for Preachers' Content of Message

DATA SHEET: TV MINISTRIES
PROGRAM ID _____ FILE # _____ CODER _____   5   SUBJECT: PREACHER CONTENT OF MESSAGE

1. In order to be saved, individual can
   a. _____ make personal decision
   b. _____ personal decision plus use of prayer, continued faith, other devotional means, self-surrender
   c. _____ personal decision, plus living Christian life (demonstrating in application Christian principles)
2. Christian Life implies that you:
   a. _____ practice in deeds Christian virtues & good works (in general, specifics not pointed out)
   b. _____ reach Christian life through art of living techniques such as power of positive thinking, in order to reach personal goals for happiness
   c. _____ live according to specific standards of right & wrong, spelled out in terms of actions & behaviors

3. a. _____ stresses need for personal security (physical, psychological well being)
   b. _____ stresses need for family security (taking care of loved ones, social & economic needs)
   c. _____ stresses need for national security (safety of U.S., threats from others)
4. When referring to signs of crisis, or manifestations of God's retribution, time for making changes is: ..
   a. _____ after death (better things promised after death)
   b. _____ here & now (fix things now to insure better life in future)
   c. _____ start now & continue to work towards better life on earth

5. In addition to concerns about individual relationships to God, other topics are mentioned. If present, note if preacher takes position, favorable or unfavorable.

TOPIC	PRO	ANTI
a. Family: traditional family patterns		
b. ERA		
c. Abortions		
d. Affirmative action		
e. Federal interference in public education		
f. Homosexuality & gay rights		
g. Censorship of school textbooks		

h. other: _____

DATA SHEET: TV MINISTRIES
PROGRAM ID _____ FILE # _____ CODER _____   5   SUBJECT: PREACHER CONTENT OF MESSAGE CONT.

6. SOURCES OF SOCIETY'S PROBLEMS MENTIONED:

a. big government _____	e. communists _____
b. the media _____	f. secular humanists _____
c. materialism _____	g. the devil, occult _____
d. denominational _____	h. other _____

7. WHAT IS NEEDED NOW, TO INFLUENCE & CHANGE THE SITUATION, IS:

a. old fashioned revival (renewal, repentance, return to God) _____
b. for you to have faith (know you are loved) _____
c. for you to join crusade to spread Biblical morality _____
d. for you to influence political process _____
e. for you to support use of applied (hard & soft) scientific technology together with religion to solve problem _____
f. individual to take active control, to influence change over self _____
g. other _____

8. COMMENTS

TOPIC	PRO	ANTI
9. DOMESTIC ISSUES: CONCERN ABOUT GENERAL DOMESTIC SITUATION		
10. gun control		
11. labor unions		
12. government regulation		
13. tax cut		
14. open immigration		
15. inflation		
16. conservation of natural resources		
17. return to old fashioned patriotism		
18. return to old truths & verities		
19. death penalty		
20. INTERNATIONAL & FOREIGN POLICY: SAVE WORLD FROM SOVIET DOMINATION & CONTROL		
21. recognition of Red China		
22. OTHER:		

Appendix C
FACTOR ANALYSIS METHODOLOGY AND RESULTS

Factor Analysis

Those items with sufficient data were submitted for principal factor analysis.

After a principal factor analysis, a narrowed pool of items was submitted for PA_2 factor analysis, varimax rotated. This PA_2 solution indicated three factors—television imperatives, charismatic leadership, and fundamentalism—accounting for 65.8 percent of the total variance in observed television behaviors (see table 10). The items showing the clearest and highest loading (.5 or higher) on a single factor were selected and used to construct additive scales; in constructing these scales, squared factor loadings and weighting procedures were followed (Bennett, 1982; Kim and Mueller, 1982).

The items or variables measure observed behaviors on the television shows. The factor analysis identifies three groups of items, each of which can be interpreted as revolving around an unknown or underlying concept (Bennett, 1982; Lazarsfeld and Barton, 1951). My interpretation of these factors and the behavioral patterns they represent is presented in the text, and it includes the results of my use of these factors as scales to ascertain variables in behavior among the television preachers (Bennett, 1982).

Table 10
Television Observations of the Electric Church Programs: Principal
Factors, Varimax Rotated
(PA_2, N Factors $= 3$)

Item—Description	Loading Factor		
	F_1	F_2	F_3
Factor 1: Television Imperatives			
Total requests made to viewer	.87		
Announcer makes request	.89		
Commercial spot format	.87		
Contact-continue watching	.69		
Total all reasons for viewer contact	.52		
Factor 2: Charismatic Leadership			
Preacher makes appeal		.74	
Appeal integrated in preaching		.79	
Total appeals to support foreign altruism		.75	
Total appeals to support charitable works		.66	
Appeals for moral crusade		.52	
Appeals for political purposes		.54	
Factor 3: Cultural Fundamentalism			
Opposes homosexuality			.66
Favors free enterprise*			.74
Favors return to old-fashioned patriotism			.77
Favors return to old truths and verities			.70
Secular topic emphasis			.88

*Note. Recode ($2 = 1$ unfavorable mention). Eigenvalues and percent variance explained for Factors (F) 1, 2, and 3 respectively: 4.65 (29.1%); 3.29 (20.6%); 2.57 (16.1%). Total explained variance $= 65.8\%$.

BIBLIOGRAPHY

Ahlstrom, S. E. (1972) A Religious History of the American People. New Haven, CT: Yale University Press.

Altheide, D., and R. Snow. (1979) Media Logic. Beverly Hills, CA: Sage Publications.

Apel, W. D. (1979) "The lost world of Billy Graham." *Review of Religious Research* 20:138–49.

Armstrong, B. (1979) The Electric Church. Nashville: Thomas Nelson Publishing.

———. (1985) "NRB in review." *Religious Broadcasting* 17 (February):66, 68.

Aron, R. (1967) Main Currents in Sociological Thought. New York: Anchor Books.

Avery, R. K. (1977) "Access and ascertainment in broadcasting." *Western Speech* 41:132–46.

Bagdikian, B. H. (1983) The Media Monopoly. Boston: Beacon Press.

Baker, R. K., and S. J. Ball. (1969) "Mass media and violence XI, report to National Commission on Causes and Prevention of Violence." U.S. Government Printing Office.

Baker, T. A., L. W. Moreland, and R. P. Sheed. (1982) "Fundamentalist beliefs and political attitudes: a study of Southern State Party Activitists." Paper presented at the annual meeting of the Society for the Scientific Study of Religion, Providence, Rhode Island, Oct. 22–24.

Bakker, J. (1976) Move That Mountain. Plainfield, NJ: Logos International.

Barnouw, E. (1978) The Sponsor: Notes on a Modern Potentate. New York: Oxford University Press.

Barton, M. (1979) "What a friend they have in Jesus." *Christian Century* 96:886–88.

Beharrell, P., H. Davis, J. Eldridge, J. Hewitt, J. Oddie, G. Philio, P. Walton, and B. Winston. (1976) Bad News. London: Routledge and Kegan Paul.

Beharrell, P. et al. (1980) More Bad News. London: Routledge and Kegan Paul.

Bell, D., ed. (1963) The Radical Right. Garden City, NY: Doubleday.

Bellah, R. N. (1975) The Broken Covenant: American Civil Religion in Time of Trial. New York: Seabury Press.

Bellah, R. N., and P. E. Hammond. (1980) Varieties of Civil Religion. Cambridge, MA: Harper and Row.

Bendix, R. (1962) Max Weber: An Intellectual Portrait. Garden City, NY: Doubleday.

————. (1968) "Max Weber." *International Encyclopedia of the Social Sciences* 16:495–502.

Bennett, S. (1982) "Construction of multi-item scales." Unpublished memo.

Berelson, B. (1952) Content Analyses in Communication Research. Glencoe, IL: Free Press.

Berger, J. (1972) Ways of Seeing. London: British Broadcasting Corp. and Penguin Books.

Berger, P. L., and T. Luckmann. (1967) The Social Construction of Reality. Garden City, NY: Anchor Books.

Bleum, A. W. (1969) Religious TV Programs: A Study of Relevance. New York: Hastings House.

Boles, J. B. (1972) The Great Revival 1787–1805: The Origins of the Southern Evangelical Mind. Lexington, KY: University Press of Kentucky.

Braverman, H. (1974) Labor and Monopoly Capital. New York: Monthly Review Press.

Budd, R. W., R. K. Thorp, and L. Donohew. (1967) Content Analysis of Communications. New York: Macmillan.

Buddenbaum, J. M. (1981) "Characteristics and media-related needs of the audience for religious TV." *Journalism Quarterly* 58:266–72.

Burns, T. (1979) The BBC. Public Institution and Private World. London: Macmillan.

Busch, H. T., and T. Landeck. (1980) The Making of a Television Commercial. New York: Macmillan.

Cantor, M. G. (1980) Prime Time Television: Content and Control. Beverly Hills, CA: Sage Publications.

Carpenter, J. A. (1980) "Fundamentalist institutions and the rise of evangelical protestantism 1929–1942." *Church History* 49:62–75.

Cartwright, D. P. (1953) "Analyses of qualitative material." In Research Methods in the Behavioral Sciences, edited by L. Festinger and D. Katz 421–70. New York: Dryden Press.

Cassata, M. B., and M. K. Asante. (1979) Mass Communication: Principles and Practices. New York: Macmillan.

Chandler, A. D., Jr. (1977) The Visible Hand: The Managerial Revolution in American Business. Cambridge, MA: Belknap Press of Harvard University Press.

Clark, D. W., and P. H. Virts. (1985) "Religious Television Audiences: A New Development in Measuring Audience Size." Paper presented at the annual meeting of the Society for the Scientific Study of Religion, Savannah, GA, October 25.

Clark, K. R. (1985) "The $70 miracle named CBN." *Chicago Tribune* (June 26) section 5:1, 3.

Cole, B., and M. Oettinger. (1978a) "Electronic church: religious broadcasting becomes big business spreading across U.S." *Wall Street Journal*, 19 May.

———. (1978b) Reluctant Regulators: The FCC and the Broadcast Audience. Rev. ed. Reading, MA: Addison-Wesley Publishing.

Comstock, G., and G. Lindsey. (1975) TV and Human Behavior: Key Studies Research Horizon Guide to the Pertinent Scientific Literature. Santa Monica, CA: Rand.

Comstock, G. (1978) "The impact of T.V. on American institutions." *Journal of Communications* 28:12–28.

Crawford, A. (1980) Thunder on the Right. New York: Pantheon Books.

Davenport, F. M. (1905) Primitive Traits in Religious Revivals: A Study in Mental and Social Evolution. New York: Macmillan.

DeFleur, M. L., and S. Ball-Rokeach. (1977) Theories of Mass Communication. 3rd ed. New York: Longman.

Durkheim, E., (1965) The Elementary Forms of the Religious Life. Trans. J. Swain. New York: The Free Press.

Eisenstadt, S. N. (1968) "Social institutions." *International Encyclopedia of the Social Sciences* 14:409–29.

Eisenstein, S. M. (1942) The Film Sense. New York: Harcourt, Brace, and World.

———. (1949) Film Form: Essays in Film Theory. Ed. and trans. J. Leyda. New York: Harcourt, Brace, and World.

———. (1970) Film Essays and A Lecture. New York: Praeger.

Ellens, J. H. (1974) Models of Religious Broadcasting. Grand Rapids, MI: W. B. Erdmans.

Elliott, P. (1973) The Making of a Television Series: A Case Study in the Sociology of Culture. New York: Hastings House Publishers.

Elliot, P., and D. Chaney. (1969) "A sociological framework for the study of television production." *Sociological Review* 17: 355–76.

Ellis, W. T. (1917) "Billy" Sunday: The Man and His Message. Philadelphia: John C. Winston.

Emery, F. E., and E. L. Trist. (1970) "Socio-technical systems." In Systems Thinking, edited by F. E. Emery, 281–96. Baltimore: Penguin Books.

Esslen, M. (1982) The Age of TV. San Francisco: W. H. Freeman.

Falwell, J. (1980) Listen America! New York: Doubleday.

Findlay, J. F., Jr. (1969) Dwight L. Moody, American Evangelist 1837–1899. Chicago: University of Chicago Press.

Finney, C. G. (1960) Lectures: On Revivals of Religion. Ed. W. G. McLoughlin. Cambridge, MA: The Belknap Press of Harvard University Press.

Fore, W. F. (1977) "Mass media's mythic world: at odds with Christian values." *The Christian Century* 94:32–38.

———. (1980a) "Equalizing access to airwaves." *The Christian Century* (April 16): 438–40.

———. (1980b) Broadcasting and the Methodist Church, 1952–1972. Unpublished diss. Ann Arbor, MI: University Microfilms International.

Frankl, R. (1984) "Television and popular religion: changes in church offerings." In New Christian Politics, edited by D. G. Bromley and A. D. Shupe. Macon, GA: Mercer University Press.

Galt, A., and L. J. Smith. (1976) Models and the Study of Social Change. New York: John Wiley and Sons.

Gasper, L. (1963) The Fundamentalist Movement. The Hague: Mouton.

Gerbner, G. (1966a) "Institutional pressures upon mass communicators." In Communication: Theory and Research, edited by L. Thayer, 205 445. Springfield: Charles C. Thomas.

———. '1966b) "An institutional approach to mass communications research." In Communication: Theory and Research, edited by L. Thayer, 429. Springfield: Charles C. Thomas.

Gerbner, G. et al. (1969) Analysis of Communication Content Developments in Scientific Theories and Computer Techniques. New York: John Wiley and Sons.

Gerbner, G., and L. Gross. (1975) "Television as enculturation—a new research approach." Unpublished paper.

Gerbner, G., L. Gross, S. Hoover, M. Morgan, N. Signorilli, H. Cotugno, and R. Wuthnow. (1984) Religion and Television: A Research Report by the Annenberg School of Communications. Philadelphia: University of Pennsylvania and The Gallup Organization.

Gessner, R. (1968) Moving Image: A Guide to Cinematic Literacy. New York: Dutton.

Gitlin, T. (1979) "Prime time ideology: the hegemonic process in television entertainment." *Social Problems* 26, 3 (February): 251–65.

———. (1980) The Whole World is Watching. Berkeley: University of California Press.

Glaser, B. G., and A. L. Strauss. (1967) The Discovery of Grounded Theory: Strategies for Qualitative Research. Chicago: Aldine.

Goldsen, R. K. (1977) The Show and Tell Machine: How Television Works and Works You Over. New York: Dial Press.

Gottschalk, L. A., C. N. Winget, and G. C. Gleser. (1969) "A manual of instructions for using the Gottschalk-Gleser content analysis scales:

anxiety, hostility, and social alienation-personal disorganization." In Training Technicians for Coding and Scoring Content, 17–35. Berkeley: University of California Press.

Gouldner, A. W. (1960) "The norm of reciprocity: a preliminary statement." *American Sociological Review* 25:161–78.

Gusfield, J. R. (1976) Symbolic Crusade. Urbana: University of Illinois.

Guth, J. L. (1983) "The new Christian right." In The New Christian Right, edited by R. Liebman and R. Wuthnow, 31–45. New York: Aldine Publishing.

Hacker, L. M. (1940) The Triumph of American Capitalism. New York: Simon and Schuster.

Hadden, J. K. (1980a) "Soul saving via video." *Christian Century* (May): 609–13.

———. (1980b) "Some sociological reflections on the electronic church." Paper presented at Electronic Church Consultation, New York University, Feb. 6–7.

———. (1985) "Religious Broadcasting and the Mobilization of the New Christian Right." Address delivered to the Society for the Scientific Study of Religion, October 26, Savannah, GA.

Hadden, J. K., and C. E. Swann. (1981) Prime Time Preachers: The Rising Power of Televangelism. Reading, MA: Addison-Wesley Publishing.

Hammond, J. L. (1979) The Politics of Benevolence: Revival Religion and American Voting Behavior. Norwood, NJ: Ablex Publishing.

Herberg, W. (1960) Protestant Catholic Jew. Rev. ed. Garden City, NY: Anchor Books.

Himmelstein, J. (1983) "The new right." In The New Christian Right, edited by R. Liebman and R. Wuthnow, 13–30. New York: Aldine Publishing.

Hofstadter, R. (1970) Anti-Intellectualism in American Life. New York: Alfred A. Knopf.

Hoge, D., P. Everett, and G. Klever. (1978) "Theology as a source of disagreement about Protestant church goals and priorities." *Review of Religious Research* 19:116–38.

Holsti, O. R. (1969) Content Analysis for the Social Sciences and Humanities. Reading, MA: Addison-Wesley Publishing.

Hunter, J. D. (1983) American Evangelicalism. New Brunswick, NJ: Rutgers University Press.

Johnson, B. (1971) "Church and sect revisited." *Journal for the Scientific Study of Religion* 10:124–37.

Johnson, J. E. (1979) "Charles G. Finney and a theology of revivalism." *Church History* 38:338–58.

Johnson, P. E. (1978) Shopkeeper's Millennium. New York: Hill and Wang.

Jorstad, E. (1970) Politics of Doomsday: Fundamentalists of the Far Right. Nashville: Abingdon Press.

Katz, E., et al. (1969) "Petitions and prayers: a method for the content analyses of persuasive appeals." *Social Forces* 47:447–63.

Kim, J. O., and C. W. Mueller. (1982) Introduction to Factor Analysis. Beverly Hills, CA: Sage Publications.

Krippendorff, K. (1980) Content Analysis. An Introduction to Its Methodology. Beverly Hills, CA: Sage Publications.

Lacey, L. J. (1978) "The Electric Church: an FCC established institution?" *Federal Communications Law Journal* 31: 235–75.

LaHaye, T. (1980) The Battle for the Mind. Old Tappan, NJ: Fleming and Revell.

Latus, M. A. (1982) "Mobilizing Christians for political action: campaigning with God on your side." Paper presented at the annual meeting of the Society for the Scientific Study of Religion. Providence, RI, Oct. 22–24.

Lazarsfeld, P. F., and A. H. Barton. (1951) "Qualitative measurement in social sciences: classification, typologues, and indices." In The Policy Sciences, edited by D. Lerner and H. D. Lasswell, 155–92. Stanford: Stanford University Press.

Lazarsfeld, P. F. (1972) Qualitative Analysis. Boston: Allyn and Bacon.

Lewis, S. (1927) Elmer Gantry. New York: Harcourt, Brace, and Co.

Liebert, R. M. (1980) "The electronic church: a psychological perspective." Paper presented at Electronic Church Consultation, New York University, February 6–7.

Liebman, R. C., and R. Wuthnow, eds. (1983) The New Christian Right: Mobilization and Legitimation. New York: Aldine Publishing.

Lloyd, M. L. (1980) A descriptive analysis of the syndicated religious television programs of Jerry Falwell, Rex Humbard, and Oral Roberts. Unpublished diss. University Microfilms.

McBrien, R. (1980) "The electronic church: a Catholic theologian's perspective." Paper presented at Electronic Church Consultation, New York University, Feb. 6–7.

McCain, T. A., J. Chilberg, and J. Wakshlag. (1977) "The effect of camera angle in source credibility and attraction." *Journal of Broadcasting* 21:35–46.

McCarthy, E. J. (1978) Basic Marketing. 6th ed. Homewood, IL: Richard D. Irwin.

McCloskey, R. G. (1951) American Conservatism in the Age of Enterprise. Cambridge, MA: Harvard University Press.

McEvoy, J. (1971) Radicals or Conservatives: The Contemporary American Right. Chicago: Rand McNally.

McLaughlin, B. (1969) Studies in Social Movements. Toronto: The Free Press.

McLoughlin, W. G., Jr. (1955) Billy Sunday Was His Real Name. Chicago: University of Chicago Press.

————. (1959) Modern Revivalism. New York: The Ronald Press.

————. (1978) Revivals, Awakenings, and Reform. Chicago: University of Chicago Press.

McLoughlin, W. G. ed. (1968) The American Evangelicals, 1800–1900. New York: Harper and Row.

Madsen, R. P. (1973) The Impact of Film: How Ideas are Communicated Through Cinema and Television. New York: Macmillan.

Mander, J. (1978) Four Arguments for the Elimination of Television. New York: Morrow Quill Paperbacks.

Mankiewicz, F., and J. Swerdlow. (1978) Remote Control: Television and the Manipulation of American Life. New York: Times Books.

Mannheim, K. (1936) Ideology and Utopia, An Introduction to the Sociology of Knowledge. New York: Harcourt, Brace, and World.

Marcuse, H. (1966) One Dimensional Man. Boston: Beacon Press.

Mariani, J. (1979) "Television evangelism milking the flock." *Saturday Review* (February 3): 22–25.

Markoff, J., G. Shapiro, and S. Weitman. (1974) "Toward the integration of content analysis and general methodology." In Sociological Methodology 1975, edited by D. R. Heise, 1–58. San Francisco: Jossey-Bass Publishers.

Marsden, G. (1980) Fundamentalism and American Culture: The Shaping of Twentieth-Century Evangelicalism 1870–1925. Oxford, England: Oxford University Press.

Martin, W. (1980) "The birth of a media myth." *Atlantic Monthly* 45 (June): 7, 10–11, 16.

Marty, M. E. (1982) "Religion in America since mid-century." *Daedalus* (Winter): 149–63.

Mathews, D. (1980) "Commercial religion and public interest." Paper presented at Electronic Church Consultation, New York University, Feb. 6–7.

Mead, G. H. (1974) Mind, Self, and Society From the Standpoint of a Social Behaviorist. Ed. C. W. Morris. Chicago: University of Chicago Press.

Merrill, R. S. (1968) "The study of technology." *International Encyclopedia of the Social Sciences* 15:576–89.

Merton, R. K. (1946) Mass Persuasion. New York: Harper Brothers.

———. (1957) Social Theory and Social Structure. Glencoe, IL: Free Press.

Millerson, G. (1961) The Techniques of Television Production. New York: Hastings House.

Mills, C. W. (1972) The Sociological Imagination. London: Oxford University Press.

Moberg, D. O. (1962) The Church as a Social Institution. Englewood Cliffs, NJ: Prentice-Hall.

Monaco, J. (1978) Media Culture. New York: Dell Publishing.

Moody, D. L. (1876) How to conduct evangelistic services and prayer-meetings. Address by Mr. Moody. Springfield, MA: G. and C. Merriam.

Morris, J. (1973) The Preachers. New York: St. Martins Press.

Niebuhr, H. R. (1956) The Purpose of the Church and Its Ministry. New York: Harper.

———. (1975) Social Sources of Denominationalism. New York: New American Library.

Nielsen, A. C. (1981) "Ratings for syndicated devotional programs." (Mimeo.)

Owen, B., J. Beebe, and W. G. Manning, Jr. (1974) Television Economics. Lexington, MA: Lexington Books.

Parker, E. C., D. W. Barry, and D. W. Smythe. (1955) The TV-Radio Audience and Religion. New York: Harper and Brothers.

Parker, E. (1980a) "Big business in religious TV." Unpublished lecture. October 26.

————. (1980b) "Your rights in broadcasting: today's biggest government giveaway." Helen Oliver Memorial Lecture. Portland, First Congregational Church, October 26.

Parsons, T. (1949) The Structure of Social Action. New York: Free Press.

————. (1951) The Social System. New York: The Free Press.

Patel, K., D. Pilant, and G. Rose. (1982) "The politics of the new Christian right: a study of Born-Again Christians in a border state." Paper presented at the annual meeting of the Society for the Scientific Study of Religion, Providence, RI, October 22–24.

Pavalko, R. M. (1971) Sociology of Occupations and Professions. Itasca, IL: Peacock Publishers.

Pope, L. (1942) Millhands and Preachers: A Study of Gastonia. New Haven, CT: Yale University Press.

Powdermaker, H. (1950) Hollywood, the Dream Factory. Boston: Little, Brown, and Co.

Pritchard, L. K. (1976) "Religious change in nineteenth-century America." In New Religious Consciousness, edited by C. Y. Glock and R. Bellah. Berkeley: University of California Press.

Quebedeaux, R. (1978) The Worldly Evangelicals. San Francisco: Harper and Row.

Reardon, K. K. (1981) Persuasion: Theory and Context. Beverly Hills, CA: Sage Publications.

Robison, J., and J. Cox. (1980) Save America to Save the World: A Christian's Practical Guide for Stopping the Tidal Wave of Moral, Political and Economic Destruction in America. Wheaton, IL: Tyndale House Publishers.

Ross, R. D. (1982) "Direct mail and the new right." Paper presented at the annual meeting for the Scientific Study of Religion, Providence, RI, October 22–24.

Schatzman, L., and A. Strauss. (1973) Field Research: Strategies for a Natural Sociology. Englewood Cliffs, NJ: Prentice-Hall.

Scherer, R. P. (1980) American Denominational Organization: A Sociological View. Pasadena, CA: William Carey.

Schneider, L., and S. M. Dornbusch. (1958) Popular Religion: Inspirational Books in America. Chicago: University of Chicago Press.

Schutz, W. C. (1958) "On categorizing qualitative data in content analysis." *Public Opinion Quarterly* 22:503–15.

Sholes, J. (1979) Give Me That Prime-Time Religion. Oklahoma: Oklahoma Book Publishing.

Shupe, A., and W. A. Stacey. (1982) Born Again Politics and the Moral Majority: What Social Surveys Really Show. New York: Edwin Mellen Press.

Sizer, S. (1978) Gospel Hymns and Social Religion: The Rhetoric of 19th Century Revivalism. Philadelphia: Temple University Press.

―――. (1979) "Politics and apolitical religion. The great urban revivals of the late nineteenth century." *Church History* 48:51–98.

Skornia, H. J. (1965) Television and Society. New York: McGraw-Hill.

Smith, T. (1958) Revivalism and Social Reform. Nashville: Abingdon Press.

Stacey, E., and A. Shupe. (1982) "Correlates of support for 'The Electronic Church.'" *Journal for the Scientific Study of Religion* 21:291–303.

Stark, R., B. D. Foster, C. Y. Glock, and H. E. Quinley. (1971) Wayward Shepherds. Prejudice and the Protestant Clergy. New York: Harper and Row.

Stinchcombe, A. L. (1978) Theoretical Methods in Social History. New York: Academic Press.

Stryker, S. (1980) Symbolic Interactionism: A Social Structural Version. Menlo Park, CA: Benjamin/Cummings.

Swann, C. (1980) "Varieties and appeals of the electronic church." Paper presented at the Electronic Church Consultation, New York University, Feb. 6–7.

Sweet, W. W. (1948) The American Churches: An Interpretation. New York: Abingdon-Cokesbury Press.

Thurmond, G. T. (1982) "Political organization of the Christian right in the south." Paper presented at the annual meeting of the Society for the Scientific Study of Religion, Providence, RI, October 22–24.

Traub, J. (1985) "CBN Counts Its Blessings." *Channels of communication* 28 (May/June): 31, 34.

Tudor, A., (1974) Image and Influence. New York: St. Martin's Press.

Wallace, A. C. (1968) "Nativism and revivalism." *International Encyclopedia of the Social Sciences* 11:75–80.

Webb, E. J., D. T. Campbell, R. D. Schwartz, and L. Sechrest. (1966) Unobtrusive Measures: Nonreactive Research in the Social Sciences. Chicago: Rand McNally College Publishing.

Weber, M. (1958) The Protestant Ethic and the Spirit of Capitalism. Trans. T. Parsons. New York: Charles Scribner's Sons.

———. (1964a) The Sociology of Religion. Boston: Beacon Press.

———. (1964b) The Theory of Social and Economic Organization. Trans. A. M. Henderson and T. Parsons. New York: The Free Press.

———. (1968) On Charisma and Institution Building. Ed. and with an introduction by S. N. Eisenstadt. Chicago: University of Chicago Press.

———. (1970) Max Weber. Ed. Dennis Wong. Englewood Cliffs, NJ: Prentice-Hall.

———. (1975) Essays in Sociology. Trans. and ed. H. H. Gerth and C. W. Mills. New York: Oxford University Press.

Weisberger, B. A. (1958) They Gathered at the River: The Story of the Great Revivalists and Their Impact upon Religion in America. Boston: Little, Brown, and Co.

White, E. E. (1972) Puritan Rhetoric: The Issue of Emotion in Religion. Carbondale: Southern Illinois University Press.

Williams, P. W. (1980) Popular Religion in America. Englewood Cliffs, NJ: Prentice-Hall.

Williams, R. (1975) Television: Technology and Cultural Form. New York: Schocken Books.

Wright, C. R. (1975) Mass Communication: A Sociological Perspective. 2nd ed. New York: Random House.

Wurtzel, A. (1979) Television Productions. New York: McGraw-Hill.

Interviews

Carlson, C. (1981) Assistant to the producer, Hour of Power, Garden Grove, CA, March 23.

George, P. (1981) Director, Traco Corp., Tulsa, Oklahoma, November 16.

Hurdle, C. (1981) Associate producer, James Robison Evangelical Association, Fort Worth, Texas, November 18.

Jones, T. Rev. (1981) Television Evangelist, Thea Jones Evangelical Association, Philadelphia, PA.

Michael, T. A. (1981) Associate Professor of Management, School of Business Administration, Glassboro State College, October 9.

Milke, E. (1980) Graduate Assistant, Annenberg School of Communications, University of Pennsylvania.

Ostrander, R. (1981) President, Ozma Broadcast Sales, Philadelphia, PA, October 5.

Parker, E. (1980) Communications Director, United Church of Christ, New York, June 11.

Shoubin, S. (1982) Program Director WPHL, TV 17, Philadelphia, PA, June 28.

Waisanan, T. (1981) Marketing Associate, Hour of Power, Garden Grove, CA, March 23.

INDEX

RAZELLE FRANKL received her Ph.D. in sociology in 1984 from Bryn Mawr College. She is currently Assistant Professor and Coordinator of Human Resources Management in the School of Business Administration, Glassboro State College, Glassboro, New Jersey. Her article "Television and Popular Religion: Changes in Church Offerings" appeared in *New Christian Politics*, edited by David Bromley and Anson Shupe (Mercer University Press, 1984).